RUNNING AWAY WITH THE CIRCUS

(or, "Now is the Winter of our Missing Tent")

By Mel Atkey

Friendlysong Books

Vancouver ● London

Published by The Friendlysong Company, Inc.
4827 Georgia Street, Delta, British Columbia, Canada
V4K 2T1

Cataloguing:

    Atkey, Mel (1958-)

    Running Away with the Circus (or, "Now is
    the Winter of our Missing Tent")
    ISBN 978-0-9916957-1-3

    1 – Memoir – humour – travel

Books by Mel Atkey

When We Both Got to Heaven: James Atkey Among the Anishnabek at Colpoy's Bay

Broadway North: The Dream of a Canadian Musical Theatre

A Million Miles from Broadway – Musical Theatre Beyond New York and London

Acknowledgements

When I travelled to Taiwan to work for the *American Universal Circus* in the autumn of 1997, I sent back weekly dispatches to a group of some twenty friends and colleagues in North America, Europe and South Africa. Assembled together, they formed a diary of the trip and became the basis for this book.

Some names have been changed or disguised to protect the privacy of the individuals involved. Certain illustrations (those of "Cynthia" and "Malcolm") were digitally created and do not represent actual persons.

However, while I was not privy to every detail of the circus' operation, the principal events surrounding the collapse of the *American Universal Circus* and of our dealings with Hsu Po-Yun and New Aspect are the truth as I understand it. Special thanks to David Gregory for his humour and inspiration, and to Norman Campbell, David Ellis Cox, Adriaan Gerber, Laurie Gibson and James Sherman for their letters.

Also, thanks to Tom Fagan, Julian Leese, Marie Camille Leese, Jane Elliot, Al Buchan, Ged Crefin, Rebecca Chen, Christian Utz, John Turner (*British Dictionary of Circus Biography*), Yi Hing and F. Kabayoshi, School of Oriental and African Studies; Hamish Todd, British Library and Michael Hurst, Taiwan POW Camps Memorial Association.

All photos by Mel Atkey except for the one with the cast of *O Pioneers!* on page 195 which is by Bill Beese.

Neither Hsu Po-yun nor Phillip Gandey co-operated in the writing of this book.

Table of Contents

Acknowledgements.. 4
Overture: The Time I Ran Away and Joined the Circus 7
Fanfare: Heartfelt Abandon.. 19
Introit: "Taiwan: A Displaced Odyssey.................................... 24
Act I, Scene 1: Renao... 32
Act I, Scene 2: "Ma-his-t'uan" 39
Act I, Scene 3: "Rolph Harris' Big Arse".................................. 44
Act I, Scene 4: "Daylight Wasting Time"................................. 51
Act I, Scene 5: "It Would Have Been Better If You Had Not
                Come" 57
Act I, Scene 6: "Stupid Boy" 65
Act I, Scene 7: "Another Openin', Another No Show"............. 72

Entr'acte: "Le Roi du Wonton"... 78
Act II, Scene 1: "Chinese Take-away".. 85
Act II, Scene 2: "The Banker"... 91
Act II, Scene 3: "Tonight's Word is Suicide" 95
Act II, Scene 4: "Home Sweet Whorehouse" 100
Act III, Scene 1: "Like Water For Petrol" 104
Act III, Scene 2: "Bullets Are Expensive" 114
Act III, Scene 3: "The Casanova From Casablanca" 122
Act IV, Scene 1: "Tentless in Touliu" 133
Act IV, Scene 2: "Chestnuts Roasting in an Open Sewer" 139
Act IV, Scene 3: "If This Were Any More Ironic, It Would Rust"
.... 153
Act IV, Scene 4: "How Much for Prostitution?" 160
Act V, Scene 1: "S'truth – This Place is Fulla White People!" ..164
Act V, Scene 2: "I've Grown Accustomed to this Farce".......... 168
Act V, Scene 3: "No Business Like Hsu Business" 171
Finale: "Just Because You're Paranoid Doesn't Mean There Isn't
                Somebody After You"........................ 181
Encore: "The Cockroach Farm" 188
Epilogue "Dancing Hsu's"... 193

To me
wishing you all the
best, it been beautiful
to work with you.
take care
Moonik

To Mel
Love from
Jamie And Lisa
Our Holiday Rep
'98
our taiwan
To Mel
All the best
Love Trawww

Take Care!
Look forward to
reading the book!
LOVE Rachel

To Mel
From

Dear Mel,
Wishing you all the
best for the future'
two books, We may see
you on the next tour,
then we prepare ourselves,
don't know..
Anyway, can't wait to
read the journals..
Kat + Greg

To Mel
All the best
see you on the
next tour
Jools.

All the best
Take care
Vaughan

Take care
Send me a copy
of the book when it's...

All the best
to you! Love,
Angela

MEL, THE WORLD
MORE POWERFUL THAN THE
TAIWANESE?

Overture:
"The Time I Ran Away and Joined the Circus"

A few years ago, if some clairvoyant had told me that I'd be spending my nights in a shipping container in Taiwan, guarding seven tigers, six Chihuahuas, five bears, four sea lions, three geese, two horses and a "killer dog" named Ludwig, I'd have said, "You're supposed to read the tea leaves, not smoke them."

But that was before my life all went horribly wrong.

In the winter of 1997, I was working at a London theatre, trying to support my ambition to be the next Andrew Lloyd Webber. Fifteen years earlier, one of Broadway's leading composers had told me that I had what it takes. Fifteen years later, I still believed him, in spite of all the evidence to the contrary – the many shows that had "almost" been produced, then collapsed with nothing to show for it. A "manqué" composer if there ever was one, I thought.

Then something happened that would, for a time, distract my attention. I had a "premonition" of sorts that I would meet an American woman about my age with an interest in musical theatre – my dream date. A few short weeks later, lo and behold, I received a message on my voice-mail from what appeared to be just such a person. "It was cute how Debra described you", said Cynthia. "She thought we might hit it off." My first thought was "Be careful what you wish for". Then I seemed to hear the Voice of God saying, "If you don't meet this girl, I don't see why I should keep you around." Besides, I needed some good news. Only a month before, my beloved "Nana" had passed on at the age of 101.

My previous quasi-love-life owed more to Franz Kafka – complete with paranoia – than it did to William Wordsworth. I seemed to be a magnet for the maladjusted. (After pursuing me for six months, one woman believed, like *Dona Flora and her Two Husbands*, that my function in life was to be her "buddy", to be always there for her, while some strapping Adonis fulfilled her womanly needs. She laughed and said, "Don't be silly! You're not *boyfriend* material!" Mind you, she did have an excuse for this behaviour – she was recovering from a brain tumour.)

This time it would be different, I hoped. I had heard mysterious legends of other possible outcomes – in much the same way as I had heard of the Loch Ness Monster, the Ogopogo, the Yeti, Bigfoot, Sasquatch, the Abominable Snowman and Little Green Men – but I had yet to see any evidence that any of them actually existed. But now I had arrived at a moment of truth. Was I really a blight on the landscape who should crawl into a rabbit hole, or should I take a chance on love, and thereby rejoin the human race? This latest entry certainly sounded intriguing. My friend Roy advised me, "I always encourage heartfelt abandon coupled with a fairly reliable parachute." So, I arranged to meet this woman at the stage door of the theatre where I worked.

"What would she look like?" I wondered. I had already formed a picture of her in my mind, based purely on her telephone voice. Although I knew she was in her mid-thirties, she sounded younger. She also sounded blonde. Not in a ditzy Marilyn Monroe way, but in a wholesome *California Dreamin'* way. Perhaps it was her use of words like "trip" and "rockin'".

As the day approached, I found myself sizing up people in the street, trying to guess what she might look like. "Hmm... Wouldn't mind if that were her..." When she finally poked her head in the door, I was amazed at how closely she resembled what I'd imagined. With sandy blonde hair, she could easily have passed for a decade younger than her thirty-six years. Not so beautiful as to be intimidating, but as Mother Webb says to Emily in *Our Town*, "pretty enough for all normal purposes".

When Cynthia Moore talked, her hands punched and clawed the air ferociously, resembling a catfight with only one cat. She had come to London from the States to study Shakespeare, and understood that I was an "artsy" type. She seemed pretty excited about the place, and was talking of moving here to escape from her "bourgeois" roots. The more she bubbled and gushed over some master-class or other she'd taken from a scion of the British theatrical establishment, the more dust and wind she stirred up, speaking in a stream of consciousness that left me stunned, bewildered, captivated and utterly terrified.

But there were wrinkles. The theatre where I worked closed suddenly, and I was left unemployed. Not wanting to be broke while there was any chance of dating Cynthia, I took the first job that came along – as a security guard at City Hall.

I rather grandly emphasised that this was not going to be a permanent career move for me: my work was in the "thee-a-tuh". "Aye," said John, an Irishman in his fifties who had been a security guard for "torty tree yars". John's alcohol soaked worldview was somewhat constricted. "In da tee-a-ter?", he asked with as wry an expression as he could muster. "Ya wore a sacyoraty gaard dere, wore ya?" In other words, "If yore so smaart, whot you doin' here, den?" I kept repeating to myself, "This mindless hellhole was not what I emigrated from Canada for".

"I can't understand your having to be a security guard when you have such experience in show business", said the late Norman Campbell, a Toronto friend and noted TV producer. "Is there some British attitude requiring PhD's before you can function over there? Is there something in your being a colonial?" A fellow composer with a West End musical to his credit, he added, "Nobody knows more than you do about musical theatre... It sounds like it might inspire you to write another *Yeomen of the Guard*". He went on to ask if the place where I was working had any redeeming features, "any statuary or scrolls, or is it just a soot-encrusted tomb for the intellect?" Nay on the former, yea on the latter. I wasn't just a fish out of water, I was a blue whale on the moon.

For three months, Cynthia and I went to plays every week, having dinner in a variety of different ethnic eateries, including Britain's only Tibetan restaurant. Then, at the end of it all, she only proved that the way to a man's heart was through his rib cage. I considered myself pretty "grounded", but it didn't stop me from getting a "shock" when she told me she already had a boyfriend. She thanked me for acting as her tour guide as she disappeared back to the land of the free.

So, here I was, with my brain stuck in neutral. Every day I awoke at that hitherto undiscovered hour, making a point of stopping to buy a copy of the *Times* out of sheer snobbery. I was doing a job specifically designed for those with an IQ below 100, but I wasn't giving in. This was the domain of the tabloid, where monosyllabic yobs gazed longingly at page three colour spreads of women with massive mammaries. It was no place to be nursing a broken heart. My cerebral cortex had been working overtime. I'd always been led to believe that I had Exceptional Potential – a walking talking Stephen Hawking – and this was as close to purgatory as I could come. I was now bored out of my egghead and going mad. So, every Wednesday afternoon I rushed to the newsagent's and scoured *The Stage* for something, anything, that would get me out of this Erebus.

A teacher of mine had often told me, "Expect to be surprised". When I least expected it, something akin to the parting of the Red Sea occurred. A small ad gleamed with divine providence from the job opportunities page:

"Circus Workers Required"

A flurry pulsated through me. Madness. Pure madness. And just what the practitioner ordered. This turned out to be a security appointment of a different ilk – for the *American Universal Circus* on tour in Taiwan.

Taiwan? That little thorn in Chairman Mao's side? Like joining the French Foreign Legion, I thought. For good or bad, I would have a story to tell – and for a writer, that was no small consideration. A chance to be taken seriously. I had already suffered the scorn of fellow aspiring writers because I chose to work in "musical comedy". Sneering at anything remotely melodic, they claimed "Anybody can write a ditty." Which would explain why the world was filled with millions of Irving Berlins but only one Béla Bartók. I was just lowbrow enough for *oeuvre* to mean the sound my stomach made while trying to digest this bilge.

I marched into the security office and announced proudly, "I'm off to China to join a circus." The room fell silent for a moment, until one of my fellow uniformed professionals twitted, "What as? A clown?" The French Foreign Legion line probably had more credibility.

"What is the job?" I asked Louise when I travelled to Cheshire for my interview. She paused to consider her response.

"Everybody will be expected to chip in and help out". I nodded, not so much in agreement as just to assure her that I was sentient. "Does that mean I'll learn to run lights, and things like that?" "Oh, no," she smiled. "We have people to do that." "So, what will my job be?" Her answer, as I understood it, was that I would be providing security on site. "Wans a sacyoraty gaard, allays a sacyoraty gaard," I could hear that Irishman drawl.

Was this one of the exciting new generation of circuses, like *Archaos* and *Cirque du Soleil*? Apparently not. No, this was a deeply politically incorrect traditional animal circus. Did I have any problem with that? To be honest, I hadn't thought about it. Would I be looking after them? "No," she said, "they have grooms for that." She continued, "You'll be keeping intruders away." "But," I pointed out, "I don't speak Chinese." That didn't matter, she told me. Yes, they had people for that too.

So, what did she want to ask me? She smiled again, looking down at my CV. "Nothing, really", she said with all the discernment of a man-hungry spinster. "It's all here." So – ? It couldn't really be this easy, could it? "Well," she explained, "the people in Taipei have to give the final approval, but..."

Let me get this straight. They're going to fly me all the way to Taiwan to be a security guard? And they're not even going to ask any questions? By what criteria were they selecting people? "I liked your accent," she said. My accent? "You sound American." Yeah, lady, just like you sound Australian.

It was my turn now to ask some tough questions. "What would happen if the show folded?" She smiled and assured me that my fears were groundless. This was a big company. Huge, in fact. And with a proven track record. She warned me, however, that it was only fair that anybody who chose not to stick it out would have to pay his or her own way home. After all, it would not be a free holiday. "And", I asked with a wry grin, "what if we get there and discover that this is a front for a white slavery operation?" She laughed nervously.

While she didn't explicitly say that I had the job, it was clear that these beggars were not about to become choosers. And why was this? She shrugged her shoulders. "I guess a lot of people don't want to be away from home for six months." "That's nothing", I said, "I've been away from home for six years."

I certainly had something to think about as I caught the train back to London. Tigger, a teasingly vivacious Irish redhead in her early thirties who was to be the wardrobe mistress, was heading north, while I went south (geographically speaking, of course). "They may be a bit disorganised," she explained, sensing my apprehension from across the railway platform, "but they're okay". As a virgin to the circus business who didn't know a king-pole from a cupola, I didn't know that Phillip Gandey, the agent who had placed the ad, was but the latest in a long dynasty, presenting circuses and ice shows in tents and arenas throughout the North of England.

I received my contract in the post a few days later, and scanned through it quickly. A "Technical Support Assistant"? I had difficulty changing light bulbs, but they had to give me an impressive title in order to obtain a work permit. At $340 US per week, I needed all the social cachet I could muster. Now I would be the opposite of that apostle of British ennui John Major, who so famously ran away from a circus to join a bank.

This would either be the most brilliant thing I'd ever done, or else it would be deeply stupid. The really unsettling thing was – I liked it that way. I beg you to pardon my use of the world's most infamous split infinitive, but I was boldly going where no tunesmith had gone before. I had no agenda. I just wanted an adventure. To "expect to be surprised". (Or, as Helène Hanff, author of *84 Charing Cross Road* put it, "Nothing ever happens the way you think it will.")

According to the itinerary, over the next six months we were expected to visit Taipei, Hsinchu, Taichung, Touliu, Chia-yi, Pingtung, Tainan, Panchiao, Kaohsiung, Hualien, Taoyuan and Miao Li. The company promised to pay for all transportation, shared accommodation and medical insurance, provided that I would swear I was free of AIDS. We would receive our salary in cash each Thursday.

Phillip was only the agent. The employer was something called the "International New Aspect Cultural and Educational Foundation". This covenant was to be signed within three days or else it would become null and void. Hoping for a full analysis (and some free legal advice), I showed the contract to a friend of mine who had a law degree. He glanced at it, then threw it down on his desk. "Sure", he said, "why not?"

"What will you do if you're stranded three quarters of the way around the world?" my father Ken inquired. "That's simple," I explained. "I'll just swim the other quarter." That did not placate him, so just in case, I had the address of the Canadian Trade Office – the nearest thing to an embassy – in Taipei.

As a precaution, I arranged a special overdraft facility with my bank, in case of any delay in remitting my money home. (This would turn out to be a wise move.) I also asked their advice on how to send it. They gave me a list of clearing banks in Taiwan that they dealt with.

So what did I need to take with me? Louise offered few clues. I knew I would need a transformer to run my most vital tool – my word processor – and other appliances on 110 AC. What else could I possibly need over the next six months? I knew nothing about the climate, so I packed a summer jacket, a winter coat, short sleeved shirts, seven (count 'em) long sleeved dress shirts, black trousers, dress shoes, sweaters and every combination in between.

Fanfare:
HeartFeLt AbaNdoN

I arrived with all my impedimenta at Heathrow Airport Terminal Four at ten o'clock on the morning of Sunday, 12 October 1997. Coincidentally, this was the date that the fictional Space Family Robinson blasted off from Earth in the 1960s sci-fi TV series *Lost in Space*. I can't say I wasn't warned.

I was on time. Where the hell was everyone else? After a while, the girl at the check-in counter directed me toward a young man wearing a sun visor standing by several metal flight-cases. I introduced myself to Al, the lighting designer who had worked for circuses and rock shows all over the world. Good, I thought. An old hand who was bound to know what we were in for, I (mistakenly) thought.

Others arrived, gradually. A pretty strawberry blonde in dreadlocks kissed a pony-tailed man goodbye, then joined us. Alice would be one of our popcorn sellers. With his waist length hair and beard, Martin, one of the tent crew, resembled a gnome. Then I spotted Tigger, the wardrobe mistress. A group of exotically dressed Arabs came in together. They were "Aladdin", a troupe of tumblers from Morocco.

In total, some thirty of us were heading for points unknown, with no idea what we were in for. I suppose, like me, each had his/her reasons.

Louise was there to hand out our travel documents. According to my ticket, I was now called "Miss Atkey". I hadn't even started, and already I'd gone from clown to bearded lady. Then I looked in my passport. I thought I might have found some welcoming coupons with my working visa, but instead found a death threat –

"WARNING: DRUG TRAFFICKING IS PUNISHABLE BY DEATH ACCORDING TO THE CRIMINAL LAWS OF THE REPUBLIC OF CHINA."

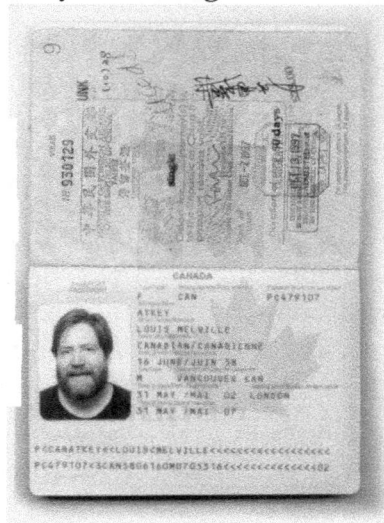

Oh, well.   Nothing to worry about. I didn't even take Aspirin.

I placed my passport into a leather pouch, which I wore around my neck.   This one was particularly valuable, as it allowed its bearer to work in three countries – Taiwan, the UK and Canada.   I would never take it off, except to sleep.

When I checked my luggage, the clerk asked if I had any new electrical appliances.   To everyone's annoyance, I answered "yes" – the adapter for my all-important word processor.   My bags had to be opened and my transformer inspected.

Following this short delay, we left on KLM for Amsterdam Schiphol Airport.   I was seated next to Paul, a circus veteran of some twenty years. I told him I'd checked it all out and believed that everything was kosher.   "Really?" he said with alarmingly arched eyebrows.

After three hours we changed planes at Amsterdam Schiphol, where I tried unsuccessfully to relive a transcendental experience I'd had with Dutch chocolate in 1992.   Then it was on to Bangkok, Thailand.   I was the only non-smoker in our contingent, yet everybody was placed in the "No Smoking" section.   For the next twelve hours, that made for an ebullient band of campers.

Looking out the window, I tried to imagine some sort of musical opening number for this unfolding extravaganza. The bevy of wing-walking beauties made famous by *Flying Down to Rio* were notable by their absence. Not even *Tap Dancing in Taipei*. Oh dear. Just a wing with engines on it. This was a disappointment.

I settled back to enjoy the in-flight entertainment, beginning with a documentary on Sir Ernest Shackleton, the explorer who led a party of twenty-six men to Antarctica, where their ship sank and they were stranded on an ice-flow for eighteen months. Then came the main feature, *Not Without My Children* starring Sally Field as a mother who travels with her family to Iran, only to have her children abducted by relatives who plan to raise them as strict Muslims.

We flew over Russia, India, Cambodia and Viet Nam – each of them an interesting place to get stranded. Those accustomed to the London Underground would expect to hear an announcement saying, "This flight will be terminating at a point 150 km north-east of Little Andaman in the Indian Ocean. Passengers are requested to make alternative arrangements for their onward journeys. We apologise for any inconvenience." But luckily, this was not the "tube".

The pilot announced that we were over Mount Everest, but I couldn't see it. I decided then that flying was my favourite mode of transport – right behind train, ship, bus and being fired out of a cannon.

I bought some film in the duty free shop at Bangkok's Don Muang Airport. My credit card statement would show that I was in four countries in different parts of the globe on the same day. (I was grateful for any pleasures, however trivial.) Then we continued on for another three hours. Next stop? Taipei.

Introit:

Taiwan:

a displaced odyssey

The heavily armed customs officer eyed me suspiciously as he inspected my passport and visa on arrival at Chiang Kai-shek International Airport. Remembering the "death threat", I remained silent. Until fairly recently, Taiwan had been a police state, and I imagined that the same people could still be running things at his level. Espying my winter clothing, he snickered, and then stamped my visa, waiving me through. I didn't have anything to worry about – so long as he didn't look at the label of my jacket, which was made across the water in the Peoples' Republic...

An attractive Chinese lady approached us, offering to satisfy any needs. As it turned out, she worked for the circus promoters, New Aspect, but that was not the first thought that crossed my mind.

Stepping outside, it may have been October, but the temperature was in the high twenties Celsius. Due to the paucity of information supplied by Louise, I had brought everything. My suitcases weighed more than Al's flight cases, and his contained lighting gear.

We scrambled aboard a coach, which after an hour or so on the Sun Yat-sen Freeway dropped us off at a hotel called the *Champagne Concierge*, located in a side lane off Sung Chiang Rd in Wenhua District. New Aspect was able to get accommodation at a bargain price because the city of Taipei had tightened its "licensing" laws.

Yes folks, that's right. Our hotel was a brothel. Which explained the mirror on my ceiling. I lay staring at myself in it, imagining that I was Martin Sheen in *Apocalypse Now*, contemplating my mission.

Then I spotted an intriguing sign on the wall, somehow related to the safety drill. It appeared to show a woman hanging out of the window. In case of police raid, perhaps? Another notice said, in English:

1. Please keep calm and listen to the instructions given from the broadcasting system.

2. Stay away from the windows.

3. Please put out your cigarettes.

4. Please do not use the elevator.

5. Turn off the main switch in the room.

Only the last sentence gave any clue as to why I should do any of these things:

6. When the earthquake has subsided, please follow the instructions given by our staff.

Martin the Gnome was in the room opposite, along with Paul, the fellow with whom I'd sat on the plane. Greg and Gedda – two friends who shared a house together in Leeds – were down the hall. Somehow, by some splendid happenstance, I had a room to myself.

Once we'd checked in, we were ordered to attend a production meeting at another nearby hotel. No consideration was given to the fact that we'd been travelling for some eighteen hours. Thirty tired and grumpy people were crammed into the gaudiest VIP suite I had ever seen (it had its own waterfall) waiting for the people from New Aspect to turn up.

We waited. We stared at the waterfall. We waited some more. Hsu (pronounced "shoe") Po-Yun, a man of fifty-three with a hairstyle that twenty years earlier might have been considered "mod", greeted us in halting English. "Welcome to China" he told us. While it sounded like a perfectly innocuous greeting, his words were chosen carefully, and with an implied political portent.

Then he invited each person to introduce him or herself. Greg, Gedda, Jools, Vaughan, Chris, Marie... When he came to Kat, who was of Filipino descent, he stopped. "You are Chinese?" he asked. "No," she said emphatically, "I'm British." "You speak Chinese?" "No." He was baffled. Since

Taiwan is a more or less racially homogenous country, I guess he expected all of us all to be white.

I learned later that Mr. Hsu was a self-taught composer of some local renown. Born in Tokyo in 1944 to Taiwanese parents during the Japanese occupation, his grandfather Hsu-Ping, an industrialist with mining interests in Korea, was a Peking Opera fan who had been a councillor assigned by the Japanese Governor-General to his "Sotokofu Hyogikai" Council in 1930 to represent Taiwan. In 1945, Hsu Ping was made a member of the Japanese parliament and was elevated to the house of peers just before the end of the occupation. His son Hsu Po-yen, a fan of western Classical music, was a very close friend of Chiang Chinkuo, son of Chiang Kai-shek. Hsu Po-yun, the grandson, even had an English great-great-grandparent.

As he was growing up in Taipei, Hsu Po-yun attended Chienkuo High School, next door to the American Cultural Centre, where he was exposed to Western ideas during a time of censorship. Or, as he told one journalist, he went there to see the "gorgeous women who worked there."[1] He was tutored from the age of sixteen by Hsu Tsang-houei, the "father of Taiwanese music", and learned to play the violin. His family connections helped him to mingle with the elite, as did his marriage to Feng Nan-ming, a noted flautist and the daughter of a high ranking general.

---

[1] *Taipei Times*, 11 October 1999

In spite of the fact that he never attended university, he was a dilettante, working variously as an architect – he had designed a couple of golf courses – a television producer and a journalist. In addition to Mandarin, he spoke Japanese, English and French. In fact, his given name meant "widely learned". Cheng Pao-Chuen wrote in *Free China Review*, "If some nosy magazine were to conduct a public vote on the ten most attractive men... or men of talent... or popular male celebrities, or major representatives of social opinion, Hsu would be a natural nominee in each category."[2] On the surface, it seemed we had much in common. His company New Aspect had been responsible for some seventy-two percent of all foreign performing arts in Taiwan.

Taking advantage of this captive mostly British audience, he explained that the Republic of China was the legitimate government of all China, and that he was disappointed when Britain handed Hong Kong to Beijing rather than to Taipei. To Hsu and his compatriots, the Crown Colony had been a buffer between his island home and an increasingly belligerent China. He felt genuinely betrayed. (Years later, he would become one of the leaders of a campaign to depose pro-independence President Chen Shui-bian, to which end he was accused of working with the Mainland Chinese.)[3]

---

[2] Chang Pao-Chuen, "Hsu Po-yun, the ROC's Impressario of the Arts", *Free China Review*, Vol. 35, No. 4, April 1985, p. 56
[3] "Anti-Chen campaigner visiting China on special mission: DPP", *China Post*, Taipei, 24 September 2006.

But we were in no mood to hear a lecture on geo-political events, no matter how ominous they may prove to be. We hoped he would tell us what we would be doing in the morning, but he only said not to worry about the animal rights protesters.

Say again? Protesters? Evidently, a Buddhist Master named Wu-hung Bhiksu was getting very hot under the collar, and getting a lot of press too. When the *Great European Circus* visited a few months earlier under New Aspect's sponsorship, Wu-hung's Life Conservationist Association accused them of exploiting numerous endangered species and exhorted the public to "reject watch the circus"[4]. "They hopefully won't get too violent", Hsu said.

Among New Aspect's staff was a formidably plump girl in her mid twenties, wearing a T-shirt emblazoned with the *Cirque du Soleil* logo. Yi, who would be the front of house manager, had spent four years in the U.S. working for *Cirque* on tour, and spoke fluent English with an American accent. We later learned that she was Mr. Hsu's niece, but at the time, we were so startled to find a Taiwanese person who spoke English like a native that we were inclined to embrace her as one of us. "Is anybody interested in going out to a bar?" she inquired.

While the others quaffed beer, I drank unsweetened Thai coconut juice. Despite my "dry" choice, I continued to hover in a kind of semi-catatonic haze not unlike the one caused by forest

---

[4] www.lca.org.tw

fires in Indonesia that had obscured our view of much of south-east Asia.

As we waited for our orders, I asked Paul, who had worked as both a technician and a performer in big tops all over Europe for over twenty years, why they'd hired theatre people instead of seasoned circus pros. With a wry wit that was at once casual and world weary, he explained that "if they had the usual circus lot here, they'd have destroyed the hotel by now and thrown each other out the window."

Paul spoke in a voice that reminded me vaguely of a cross between the Bristol-tinged delivery of Cary Grant and the nasal snarl of W.C. Fields. His accent was hard to place, having grown up on the road. At home in England, he lived in a trailer, which he brought to each job. This was the norm in the circus world. Hotel rooms were a luxury, he said. Divorced, he had a seventeen-year-old daughter. Although not the oldest member of our crew, Paul was, in many respects, the elder statesman. He'd seen it all, and was philosophical about it. When he spoke of circus life, he painted a picture of a notoriously rough crowd – burly men with Bluto muscles who would pound in stakes like a jackhammer, working thirty-six hours straight, then rape and pillage the town, moving on before anyone knew what had hit them. Being a community that could literally pull up stakes and move inspired some to think that they operated outside the law.

As we finished up our drinks, Yi suggested that we move on to the Snake Alley night market in Hua Hsi Street, where you could watch a live snake being disembowelled, then imbibe a kind of bile secreted from it. This was supposed to be an aphrodisiac. I couldn't wait to avoid partaking of that delicacy. While she had a few takers, I just wanted to sleep.

Ah, sleep! The thought was intoxicating. Unfortunately, for a veteran insomniac like myself, "Ah, sleep!" did not mean "a-sleep". I tossed and turned, my heart pounding with adrenaline, barely closing my eyes once.

Act One: Scene 1
"Renao"

Week One

I would love to describe this as "awakening for the first time in Taiwan", but since I had not been to sleep, I can't. While I was *trying* to sleep, some of my colleagues did the Taipei pub-crawl, finally landing in some "all-you-can-drink" inebritorium. In the morning, Simon, one of our agent's henchmen, tried to rouse them, but found no signs of life.

I might as well have joined them, for all the lucidity I possessed. I staggered into the lift and pressed "lobby". It went down, eight, seven, six, five, three, two – wait a minute. What happened to "four"? Checking my guide book, I found that the Mandarin word for "four" sounded a bit too much, for their comfort, like their word for "death", so like the number "thirteen" in Western buildings, they simply skipped it. (I suppose it was easier than inventing a new word.)

When I reached the foyer, the receptionist stopped me. "You friend call". Friend? Who knew I was here? Then I realised that I had reached the outer perimeter of her comprehension. She ushered me into an anteroom with a small Buddhist shrine and the smell of incense. Gradually the other members of our team were sent in there.

Then Phillip Gandey arrived. A slim Northerner, he was forty-one years old with a neat crop of curly brown hair and a pasted on grin. A veteran of a circus dynasty that stretched back over a century (his grandfather, Bob "Gandey" Briggs had worked in music hall), Phillip had made his debut as "Starri the clown" at the age of four, and gained nine "O" levels attending a variety of schools while on tour. He took over the show following his father's death in 1973. Initially working with other partners, he expanded the show, buying bigger tents, bringing in more animal acts, and branching out into ice shows, corporate entertainment and hosting the *Chinese State Circus*. Phillip's company "Caseload Ltd." was the agency who had recruited us.

But here in Taipei, "Starri" was not a happy clown. Phillip had heard about his new crew getting crapulous the night before, and he was having none of it. "Fellas, I'll tell you this once, and not again. If I hear of any more incidents like last night, you'll be on the next plane home."

The tent had not yet arrived from England. As we lingered on the hotel steps for want of some instructions, Greg, a theatrical stagehand from Leeds quipped in a deep Yorkshire voice, "Now is the winter of our missing tent!" This meant we were free for the rest of the day.

My first order of business was breakfast. Balking at the over-priced hotel fare, I elected instead to purchase a sort of omelette with onions called *dàn*

bĭng, rolled and sliced, from a street vendor. It was very good and, at twenty New Taiwan dollars (about forty pence), very cheap.

As I stepped out into the main streets, I was overwhelmed by the frenetic anarchy – what the Taiwanese euphemistically called *renao* or "liveliness" – of the place. Taipei was mad with motor scooters. I wondered, "Am I really here? Or am I just incredibly lost in London's Chinatown?"

For one whose livelihood involved observing Life's Rich Pageant, Taipei was May Day in Red Square, the Rose Bowl and the Santa Claus Parade all rolled into one. Wherever I went, I was blanketed by a soundscape straight out of *Blade Runner*. This was "renao". The music box tinkling that I normally associated with an ice-cream truck belonged rather disconcertingly to the rubbish removal van. The sidewalks were crowded with parked motor scooters. Drivers and pedestrians alike took aim at their destination, set a trajectory, and were mercilessly unforgiving of whatever stood in their way, be it people, parked motor bikes, food kiosks or the mongrel stray cats and dogs that littered the streets, scrounging for meals.

I have a theory about great cities. Just as a laser beam is visible only because of the impurities that reflect it, great cities seem only to show up on the radar screens of world opinion because of their conflicts and urban decay. Taipei was vibrant (or is that vibrating?) to the point of palpitations. Founded in 1879 under the Ch'ing dynasty, it was a carefully planned city. Or it might have been if the plans had actually been adhered to. With a metropolitan population of almost six million people, it was in a beautiful locale, but was not a beautiful city. Set in the mountains, where there had been an opportunity to build a Rio de Janeiro, instead they had built a Pittsburgh.

Even if lacking in aesthetics, Taipei was clearly swimming in money. There was a heavier military presence than most Westerners were used to, with numerous army barracks scattered throughout the city. One was always aware that the covetous nuclear power that lay across that narrow body of water still regarded them as a renegade province.

Soon I encountered the "Chinese whisper" version of English. A collection of randomly joined up phrases on street signs advertised a "Jungly New Pub". Another one in a shop window said "To Run Business" [open]. On the other side it said "To Drink Tea" [closed]. A large, multi-story stone building with massive Grecian columns shouted in gargantuan letters, "BARBER SHOP" (a euphemism for a brothel), while a very dour looking man walked past wearing a jacket that said "THE CROWDS GAPE WHEREVER I GOES I HAVE IN A WORD PIZZAZZ."

While the official religions were Buddhism, Taoism and Confucianism, the most prevalent appeared to be "7-Eleven"ism, with temples on every street corner, hawking everything from dried mangoes and sushi to hot coffee in a can.

The following morning, I bought my "dàn bǐng" from the same stall. The lady smiled, and although she spoke no English, she remembered me, and that little bit of familiarity was a comfort.

The New Aspect staff were anxious to put us to some constructive use. They handed us several rolls of coloured metallic tape with which to make ourselves decorous, then sent us out in taxis looking like an army of cross-dressing androids, to leaflet in front of the SOGO department store at the intersection of Chungsiao East Road and Fuhsing Road. "This does not bode well", muttered Paul, the circus veteran, looking like John Wayne in a tutu. People were prepared to risk their lives in order to avoid us.

At last, the tent arrived, and for most of the crew, the hard part had begun. I was lucky. I was given the soft option of doing the night shift.

Act I, Scene 2:
Ma-hsi-t'uan

I received my first post – a letter from my father. "I'm glad you got there okay and hope this job turns out to be an enlightening experience. I imagine most of it will be rough and tumble between putting up tents, moving from hotel to hotel, not knowing the language or the people you are working with."

Arny, a tough talking, beer bellied Geordie with an industrial strength moustache was our head of security, and I shared the duties with Vaughan and Chris. That night, Chris and I had to find our way to the site on our own. While the crew rode on the company bus, our odd schedule meant taking taxis.

Hailing a cab in Taipei was a challenge to the Mandarin-impaired, because few drivers spoke any English. I asked Yi to write out the site address for us in Chinese characters, along with a note saying, "Please give receipt." This was imperative so that we could claim back our expenses at the end of the week.

We then flagged down the yellow cab, waving a hand – or other body part – frantically. As the car stopped and the door opened, an electronic chime played a Beethoven sonata with a tonality normally associated with mobile phone ringtones. Our fares varied wildly between 100 – 500 NT (New Taiwan Dollars) for the same journey. NewAspect disputed some of these expense claims, but how were we supposed to argue with the drivers?

Simulated white-knuckle thrills were all the rage, but "Taipei Cab Ride" was the real thing. According to a guide book published by the Taipei International Women's Club, the rule of the road was "He who gets there first has the right-of-way, except in the cases where he who drives the largest vehicle claims the honour."[5]After some seven near death experiences, we arrived at the site, in a park on the south side of the Hsientsen River in Yungho City, at about eight thirty at night. A crane was depositing shipping containers, including a large flat bed carrying our tent and poles.

The site, beneath Chung-cheng Bridge, had the consistency of a sandbar. The metal towers that supported the high-tension lines that crossed the grounds were set atop enormous concrete piers at least six metres high. Hmm. Curious. There was a reason behind this, I was sure. The fish jumping in the puddles might be a clue.

We spent our first night out in the open, accompanied by a bilingual – i.e. Mandarin and Taiwanese – "interpreter". The only light came from a battery-powered torch. One of the containers would act as our workshop and shelter, but at this point it was still full of lighting instruments, so we were left out in the elements.

---

[5] *Living it Up in Taiwan*, Taipei International Women's Club, 1984, p. 143.

Like me, Chris came from the theatre, having worked back stage in the West End as a fly-man. Smallish, twiggy and bespectacled, he looked as though he would snap under the weight of a large leaf. However, there was nothing timid about him. He would rather have been part of the tent crew, even though they made less money. Sitting guarding things was boring, he thought, and I could hardly put any convincing arguments to the contrary.

At Phillip's suggestion, we took turns sleeping on the canvas bags the tent came in. Restful it was not, especially with a Chinese colleague who would practice conjugating verbs by stringing all the English words he knew into one disjointed sentence.

I sat there in the dark thinking to myself, "This sure did the trick. Why, I'm hardly thinking about Cynthia at all. Any moment now I'll be over her. Talk to me in six months' time and I won't even remember what she looked like. Yessir." Then I would recall those blue-green eyes that had burned themselves into my consciousness – the coloratura way she had of singing her yawns – and I knew that six months could be a long time.

In the morning, a mini-bus arrived to take us back to the hotel. As the driver put his key in the ignition, an electronic voice recited a lengthy repertoire of recorded messages in Mandarin that we assumed said things like "fasten seat belts" and "check oil", although one could only speculate about the significance of the cock crowing.

When I returned to the hotel, I wrote my first letters home, using an ageing word processor with a few wonky keys. (My friend Norman Campbell wrote back that he donned his Sherlock Holmes deerstalker to solve the mystery of what letters were missing.) The same letter, describing the adventure so far, went to a list of some twenty friends and colleagues in the U.K., South Africa, the U.S. and Canada. As our stops were to be brief and the mail unpredictable, I gave out Phillip's address in Cheshire for return post. Except for my family, whom I would phone every week – I gave them the hotel address.

When we arrived the following evening for our second shift, a metamorphosis had taken place. Gone was the flat bed container. In its place, like some giant toadstool that had grown up overnight out of the dewy grass, stood a circus tent. As we entered this dark grotto our voices bounced off the walls, ceiling and unfinished seats. Ladies and gentlemen, step right up…

And they did. In the morning, some locals walked straight into the tent, almost totally ignoring us, determined to do their Tai-chi on the same spot they had staked out for years. We approached them delicately.

"How much ticket?" one of them asked. We had no idea. Nobody had thought to tell us. This was just the sort of situation I was thinking of when I asked Louise "How can I be a security guard when I don't speak the language?" Yet, nobody seemed to mind. Maybe Louise's instincts had been correct. Perhaps my "American" sounding accent was part of the exotic charm of the show.

But, even without the language barrier, how could we explain what a circus was, when Taiwan (unlike Mainland China) had no such tradition? At least their word for 'circus' – *Ma-hsi-t'uan* – was fairly descriptive – "performing horse troupe" – unlike the English name, which just meant "circle".

Act I, Scene 3
Rolph Harris's Big Arse

Week Two

If the batch of correspondence I sent to my friends and colleagues back home did not reach them safely, it may have been because it was hard to tell a Chinese mailbox from a rubbish bin. (It would be another year before I would open my first email account.) First, I went to the hotel concierge and asked her where I could post my letters. She said, "I take them." Then, as I saw her put them in a big brown envelope marked "Safe Deposit Box", I snatched them back and said, "No, I take them!"

I grew up in an officially bilingual country, (meaning that we had French and English on our cereal boxes) and had travelled in lands where French, German, Italian, Spanish, Swedish, Danish, Dutch, Čzech, Erse and even Basque were spoken, but this was the first time I'd been in a place where nothing was familiar. No word, no sign meant anything to me. I kept battling an irrational urge to speak French. I was far from fluent, but compared to Mandarin, I could parlez vous Français like Voltaire.

I did manage to learn two words. "Lu" meant "road", so I could now tell the cab driver that I was looking for Sung Chiang Lu. And in the unlikely event that he delivered me there safely, I could say "hse-hse", or "thank-you".

As a foreigner twice removed, miscommunication was nothing new to me. I was still struggling to understand British accents, never mind Chinese. When I first arrived in London, a group of cockney ladies at work were discussing a picture spread in *Hello* magazine. What I overheard was, "Have you seen Rolf Harris' *arse*? It's huge!" Only after her description became more graphic – "It was propped up on stilts" and "he's having an extension added" – did I realise she was saying "house".

On the other hand, I wasn't always understood either. I once went into an Oxford Street clothing store and asked for a tuque, a vest and suspenders. The sales clerk gave me a blank stare. "A tuque?" he asked. "Do you mean a tuxedo?" No, I didn't. For the latter two items, he referred me to the underwear department[6]. After an extended game of charades, what I eventually came out with was a "woolly hat", a "waste-coat" and "braces". When somebody told me he'd been run down by a car on the pavement, I told him it served him right – he should have been walking on the sidewalk. And where I came from, only planes drove on the tarmac. We were, indeed, divided by a common language.

Every chance I got – and there weren't many – I would flee the so-called circus we were with and try

---

[6] For the latter item, read "the ladies underwear department".

to explore the real circus that was going on outside. To feed my soul. I came here to have my eyes opened. While others in the company looked for the nearest thing to an English pub to bury themselves in, I wanted to immerse myself in Taiwan.

The key to my freedom was Taiwan's railways. Unlike the buses, the destination signs were in both Chinese and English, making accessible to foreigners such as myself. I might add that, like my father (and his father before him) I am a railway enthusiast, so this posed no burden for me.

The first spare moment I had, I hopped on a train. But first I had to find one. The Taiwan Railway Administration had very cleverly hidden them. Owing to Taipei's hyper-congested streets, the government carried out a very ambitious programme to put all of the city centre's mainline tracks underground, feeding into a massive new station in Chunghsiao West Road. From there I was able to catch a commuter train over Taiwan's oldest railway line – opened in 1891 – to Keelung, a seaport on the north-east side of the island. The trains were brand new, resembling subway cars. The journey took just over half an hour.

The skyline of Keelung – Taiwan's second major seaport, behind Kaohsiung – was dominated by the 23 metre statue of Kuanyin, the Goddess of Mercy, atop a hill in Chungcheng Park. Right, I thought. I'm going up there, and I'm going to learn what this statue – the largest of its kind in Southeast

Asia – was about. It turned out that the early Taiwanese settlers revered Kuanyin – who "observes the cries of the world" – as a settler of land disputes. In fact, she was central to the Buddhist notion of "karuna", or compassion. As I approached the temple, I wondered, "How does one show respect? Am I expected to remove my shoes?" Then I found the attendant sitting in a side room watching TV, while a vending machine inside the temple sold Coca-Cola.

Nearby, I found Hainen Tienhsien, a fortress – one of the few of indigenous Chinese design – built in 1840 to defend Keelung harbour against British attacks during the Opium Wars. Local magistrate Yao Ying ordered its construction, complete with eight cannons, on a site with strategic views of the harbour. On its front gate was a tablet inscribed "This gate to the sea has been provided by Heaven for our defence". It survived three British attacks, only to succumb to the French in 1884. This was to be the only time in the entire trip when I would be able to gaze out across the Pacific Ocean in the direction of my Canadian homeland.

I took the train back to Taipei. When I got back to the hotel, I discovered another group had arrived from the U.K. Among them was a young Welshman in his late twenties whom they called Sweetpea. I gathered that he was not Gandey's first choice for this assignment, but somebody had dropped out, and they were desperate. He used to be known as "Popeye" until one of his bosses got annoyed and demoted him. Any further illumination of his background was hampered by the fact that he spoke with the elocution skills of Donald Duck.

The next morning I put a "Do Not Disturb" sign on my door, and went straight to bed. Soon my doorbell rang. Ignoring the sign, Vaughan, a big beefcake of a northerner who was to be my partner that night, invited me to go out for lunch. I was so tired, I said "yes", thinking that it really was time to get up.

We found an all-you-can-eat buffet across the street, which cost me 350 NT – About £6 – the most I had paid for a meal so far. I had a pork chop, served with a roll made of very sweet bread, and a type of fish soup that was cooked at my table. I watched the chef fry the vegetables, flinging them in the air, and catching them with my plate. It was a chance for Vaughan and I to get to know each other before we started work.

"If the show goes to Mainland China", he asked, "what'll you do?" It wasn't official, but there was talk of extending the tour after a month-long break. I suggested I wouldn't mind catching the ferry to Japan. "My uncle's in Australia," he said. "I might go there."

I casually remarked that this was a job for a single person, trying to convince myself that there was an up side to this status. Vaughan explained that he had just broken up with his girlfriend of three and a half years. Ah, something I could relate to, I thought. This flight of romanticism-cum-self-pity crashed back to Earth as he casually explained, "She was too old for me". She was thirty-nine years old. Checking my birth certificate, I noted that I was also thirty-nine. Any chance for serious camaraderie between Vaughan and I had been dealt a serious blow indeed. He continued, "The sex was fantastic, very passionate, but I just couldn't go out with someone that old". Clearly, for him a soul mate was nothing more than a missing shoe.

Act I, Scene 4
"Daylight Wasting Time"

Left to their own devices, the Taiwanese seemed somehow mysteriously to get things done. However, the moment they tried to collaborate with westerners, it all became impossible. I had to go to Taiwan to learn the meaning of the English expression "pear shaped".

Typhoon Ivan was cutting a swath across south-east Asia, and we were in its path. Its 93-mph winds had already killed one person and blown down more than eighty houses in the Philippines. Moreover, and possibly more ominously, New Aspect had failed to get planning permission for the site, which was in a flood plane. (Remember the fish I saw jumping in the puddles?) So, the tent had to come down. All of it.

I spent a moment gaping in disbelief. Then Ian, the technical director shouted, "Come on, we've got work to do." I was about to find out what Louise meant by "chipping in and helping out." In the circus, job descriptions were irrelevant. So, I would learn, were contracts. Mine was not to reason why, mine was but to do and hope I don't die.

We worked into the night, forming a "disassembly" line. We dismantled the seating, consisting of stringers (the steel forms on which the seating rested), "A frames", seating boards, benches and bucket seats. The stringers were the thickness of a steel girder. Pain and exhaustion were the order of the day – another selling point that Louise had neglected to mention in my interview. Then we packed the four thousand seats away in their correct order. I hadn't escaped the hard work after all, and boy, this was hard. Here I was, nearing forty, doing manual labour for the first time since I'd been a casual stage hand at CBC Television in Vancouver in the early eighties.

"Just do what you can," Paul said. "That's all anyone can ask." Simon, one of the few circus regulars on our crew, sneered when I couldn't lift the heavy weights. I didn't dare complain too loudly. Because Mr. Hsu decided that security was important, Vaughan, Chris and I were making half again as much as the tent crew, and – thanks to Vaughan's loose tongue – they knew it. After taking this tent down, camping would seem like such a breeze.

At midnight, when we finally knocked off, the site was left in the hands of the Chinese guards and Jim, the bus driver who was assigned to stay with us for the entire tour, drove us back to the hotel.

After a brief and restless sleep, I returned on the bus with the rest of the crew bright and early the following morning. As my bleary eyes focused, two dark figures emerged from out of the mist of obfuscation that was the New Aspect hierarchy. With his bouffant hairstyle and American bomber jacket, Ken, the production manager looked vaguely like a Taiwanese attempt at an Elvis impersonation. He seldom smiled. His English was passable, but he would rather that we all spoke Mandarin.

Ken remained aloof from us, while delegating the more pressing issues to Vincent, his site manager and side-kick. Vincent, in turn, was always shouting down his mobile phone at some faceless minion. One sensed that these two were in a constant state of "crisis management", an expression which, in this context, aspired to oxymoronic heights.

Phillip Gandey had never brought a circus to Taiwan before, although he had taken acts from there to England, working with a former partner of Mr. Hsu's. It was through this connection that our show was set up, but before it came to fruition, Mr. Hsu and this partner had fallen out.

In Taiwan, one needed to master the unique form of diplomacy called "Guanxi", which roughly means, "I scratch your back..." Showing anger suggested a lack of breeding. As Vincent was fond of dropping the names of all the nefarious characters with whom he was personally acquainted, it might, in hindsight, not have been prudent to cause him to lose face through any churlish ingratitude on our part.

Phillip asked for a six-ton fork-lift. Vincent couldn't find one, but the Chinese sense of honour precluded his coming back empty handed, so he sent a four-ton and a two-ton instead. Although Phillip was normally unflappable, I observed a gradual coarsening in his vocabulary as he queried, "How did you manage to gather all your idiots together in one place?"

All of this begged one burning question for me. Hadn't Phillip done his due diligence? Surely he checked this place out before coming over here? After all, I had enough presence of mind to ask a few straight questions (even if I didn't get straight answers). Hadn't he?

The rest of the day proceeded at a crawl, with more pauses than a Pinter play. Greg looked at his watch, then announced, in his broad Yorkshire dialect, "It is now 12:54 Daylight Wasting Time".

Paul explained to me that if this was England, a particular truck or crane would be slated for a particular time, and it would be there. But this was not England. This was Taiwan, and they don't do circuses in Taiwan. They don't have the support infrastructure. When one travels to a prairie wheat field, one doesn't complain that there are no subways and bistros.

When the required equipment failed to arrive, Phillip ordered us back on to the bus, to wait in our hotels for further instructions. After tarrying several more hours, I was dispatched back to the site, only to be sent straight home again.

The following morning, we were still struggling to get our tent down. This job should have taken a single day, but one of the cranes became stuck in the mud. When the Taiwanese workers tried to use another crane (of equal size) to pull it out, they both became stuck. Then I heard an almighty crack: one of the cranes had literally snapped in two.

This time, Phillip demanded action. Vincent replied, "Your problem be solved in one hour. In mean time, please ask people to keep emotion." We would have no difficulty doing that.

Somehow, Vincent's assurances were not taken seriously. "Do you know what an anagram for 'Taiwan' is?" Gedda suggested. "Na, wait!" He explained, "The good news is, it will take three days. The bad news is, that's Thursday of this week, Tuesday of next week and Friday the week after."

Eventually the tent did come down. Now we could draw a line under our troubles. The worst was all behind us. As Jim the bus driver transported us to the new site, we were filled with anticipation that, after a false start, we were finally in gear, and the show would go on.

"It Would Have Been Better If You Had Not Come"

How could I describe it? Cesspool? Toxic waste dumping ground? The only thing that could be said for the new site in the midst of an industrial area in Panchiao, to the west of Taipei City, was that it was vacant. A factory had recently been demolished there, and the land graded, leaving the excess dirt piled in large mounds on the perimeter of our rectangular lot.

Our first job was to drive our stakes into the concrete. Paul handed me a large mallet, and said, "Get to work." I hesitated a moment before wielding the large and uncommonly destructive implement. How hard could it be? "Anyone can do this", he said.

Just like wielding an axe. Paul held the stake while I took a swing at it, hurling the lumbering object over my head and in the general direction of Paul's wrist. Landing within a few millimetres of him, he was clearly distressed. Grabbing the mallet away from me, he glowered balefully. Clearly, I was not just anyone. Then it dawned on somebody that we could use a compressed air drill to do the job, making the whole thing a lot easier – and safer.

Building up the tent, complete with seating, was without question the hardest physical labour I had ever done, and, at thirty-nine, I was in no condition for it. My seven starched white shirts and dress trousers were obviously not going to be very useful to me here.

Raising the kingpoles was a particularly delicate operation. These four key supports were attached to guy wires. We took turns winching them up in unison, two at a time, while a crane carried the weight.

My hands were blistered by rope burns. I looked in the first aid kit for plasters, but all that I found was a packet of gravol pills. If I'd needed a triangular bandage, gauze or dressing, I would have been out of luck. Not so much as a band aid. In the theatre, a unionised and highly disciplined and regulated workplace, safety would be paramount. Here, where a snapped cable could easily sever a limb, safety was for sissies. As we debated the relative merits of wearing steel-toed work boots for protection, the Russians turned up wearing only their hotel slippers.

Through the haze of fatigue and exertion, in the thick of all the construction and muck, a table with flowers on it suddenly materialised. Had we reached T'ien, the Chinese heaven?

A monk handed us incense sticks and told us to hold them facing the sun, bending three times. Next they burned some "Ghost money"[7], and set off firecrackers. This was intended to help our ancestors in the afterlife, and thereby bring us good fortune. They weren't taking any chances this time.

As we worked, we were serenaded by a loudspeaker system disseminating propaganda to all who would listen (or to those who lacked adequate soundproofing). The site belonged to one of the candidates standing for election to Taipei County Council. Just what he stood for was anybody's guess. Sweetpea heard that he was a Communist, but that seemed unlikely, given Hsu's introductory monologue on the glories of Chiang Kai-shek's China. We were each given a sun visor with a political slogan silk-screened on it. With the hot October sun beating down on us and burning our foreheads, we were in no position to exercise censorship.

I'd been working all day without a break, and I was famished. Clearly, my needs were not going to be accommodated by the powers that be, so I

---

[7] The burning of Ghost Money – especially during July, which was Ghost month –was so widespread that it was causing serious pollution problems in Taipei, and the city was trying to restrict the practice to its municipal incinerator at Mucha.

proclaimed my own dinner break and escaped to the shop across the street. Paul told me, "You have to look after yourself. No one will do it for you."

We barely managed to hoist the king poles before nightfall. I went to Louise's hotel room to collect my wages, only to find a queue waiting outside. When she insisted that we be paid on time, Hsu fired her.

Boris, the sea lion trainer, went in first to collect for the Russians. This took about three-quarters of an hour. Then Gavin, the ringmaster, a fellow Canadian from Guelph, Ontario who had been in the business for forty-three years, arrived fortified with whiskey, and collapsed in a corner.

Yi entered the corridor outside the room and found a large group of us sitting (except for Gavin who was laying face down) on the floor. "Don't blame me", she sighed, her fleshy cheeks exaggerating her weary expression. "I haven't been paid in weeks." This was considerably more than we wanted to know at this point.

Yi was only too aware of her uncle's shortcomings. "He's only related by marriage", she emphasised. "He's not a blood relative." She added, "His wife is my mother's cousin." As the most fluent English speaker, she was our information conduit, a role with which she was not entirely comfortable.

It was well past midnight before I received my money. I made the mistake of showing Greg my pay stub, made out to "Louis Melville Atkey". My full name had, until that point, been on a strict need to know basis, but he picked up on it like a cat to fish. "Louie!" he shouted. "Hey, Louie!"

The following day I took my money to a local branch of the Hua Nan Commercial Bank and wired it home. I was still paying rent on my flat in London, and was anxious that my money went into my account each week.

For companies touring Taiwan, clearing customs was always a major ordeal, and delays were par for the course. When New Aspect brought Australia's Bangarra dance troupe to Taipei, their sets and costumes – which consisted largely of organic material – were held up, and the first night was performed "with considerable assistance from a smoke machine."[8]

The animals were greeted at the airport by protesters wearing tiger and bear masks. "We don't want the children of Taiwan to receive this kind of education", said Buddhist Master Wu-hung of the Life Conservationist Association.[9] "We don't want them to think that wild animals are only here to dress up in tutus, silly hats and roller-skates to entertain humans."

---

[8] *"Let's Tour" Case Studies*, Australia Council for the Arts, 2002.
[9] *China News*, 5 April, 1997.

The days of the animal circus were numbered. Phillip maintained that the animals in his shows were treated humanely, and an article in the March 1982 issue of *Kingpole* magazine stated that Phillip's method of giving these animals plenty of freedom between shows met with the approval of a prominent British animal protection society.[10]

Hsu's argument was arguably the more aesthetic, if logically perverse, comparing the bears to Beethoven and Mozart. "They were beaten by their fathers to become geniuses in music. And at the end, most of these artists thank their parents... Animals have the right to show their wisdom and progression by performing."[11] It made you wonder how his musical career got started.

On the other hand, Wu-hung's approach to animal rights was uncompromising. "Even if fresh water turtles are released into salt water and die, it is still better than dying in a cooking pot. In fact, they are giving the animals euthanasia."[12] He claimed that animal treatment in Taiwan resembled that in the U.S. a century earlier, before the formation of humane societies. His group was fighting an uphill battle to bring in animal rights legislation in a country where

---

[10] Jack Niblett, "The Gandey Story", *Kingpole*, #59, March 1982, p.13
[11] *China News*, ibid.
[12] *The Buddhist Perspective on Animals and Life Conservation: Their Changing Rules in Society*, lecture given by Wu-hung Bhiksu in Prague, 11/9/98.
http://online.sfsu.edu/rone/Buddhism/BuddhismAnimalsVegetarian/Buddhist%20Perspective%20on%20Animals.htm accessed 11 February 2013.

the streets were crowded with stray cats and dogs. Referring to us, he added, "It would have been better if you had not come." We were beginning to agree with him.

Act I, Scene 6
"Stupid-Boy"

Week Three

Our crew found a dead snake when they cleared out one of the rusty old shipping containers on New Aspect's storage lot. The plan was to transform these decrepit steel boxes into portable buildings. In actual fact, very little transformation was involved. A plain container with a hanging light bulb would pass as a dressing room.

The animals finally cleared quarantine, and were beginning to arrive in their tiny cages. Pointing to the tigers, Paul informed me that my job on the night shift would be to go out every hour and count them. "There should be seven", he said with a cocky smile, adding "If there aren't, then lock yourself inside the empty cage."

John Campolongo, the tiger trainer shook his head as I helped him unload his props. With his beard and bandanna, he might have stepped out of a production of *The Pirates of Penzance*. In fact, he had recently played the part of an animal trainer in a French TV movie, *La Dame du Cirque*.

"Don't worry", he told me as his golden striped "cats" thrust their claws through the bars of their flimsy cages in anxious anticipation of up to forty pounds of daily red meat. "They're a bunch of geriatrics".

John was a winner of the Silver Clown (1994) at the International Festival in Monte Carlo with some thirty years experience training lions and tigers, many of them under contract to the Hawthorne Circus Corp. of Richmond, Illinois. Among his brood of seven was a rare white tiger, produced by mating two Bengal tigers who both carried the white gene.

On this trip, his professional groom, who would have stayed with the "cats" at night, had baled out at the last minute, so wife Sharon and daughters Christina and Angela would have to help out.

In an attempt to placate Wu-hung and his protesters, Hsu had his welders rebuild some old shipping containers into larger cages for the tigers and bears. Interestingly, even in the larger space, the bears confined their movements to the dimensions of their previous cages, staring ahead and rocking back and forth. According to the animal rights activists, this was a symptom of psychological damage.

Christina, Tiger John's eldest daughter, was much younger than she looked. As a girl who had spent her entire life in circuses, I sensed that she regarded the men around her with a mixture of trepidation and fascination. This was probably justified, as with her long flowing curly auburn hair and petite figure, she "scrubbed up rather well", and circus men were not known for their reticence. She did an act on horseback, though she really wanted to be an acrobat. As they hadn't been home to

Philadelphia in three years, she studied by correspondence. Along the way, she'd picked up several languages, including French and Spanish.

Gavin sent one of the New Aspect staff to buy three dozen tennis balls for the sea lions to balance on their noses. Vincent sent another lad to fetch a roll of string with which to rope off part of the car park. Elsewhere on the lot, the crew were assembling the pool for the sea lions. This was to be filled from a large aluminium tank, kept on site. The "sea monsters" (as I called them) were kept in wheeled cages, four of them in three "shifting boxes". Their trainer, Boris Maihkrovski, a small, balding, portly man in his late thirties who resembled, well – a sea lion, was the spokesman for the Russian artists, and one of the few who spoke English.

The Russians – Yuri, Evgueni, Natalya, Galina, Sascha and company – were the most self-contained unit in the show, preparing their own meals on site. The last time I'd worked with Russian artistes – a ballet company at Sadlers' Wells – the dancers had written the combination numbers for their dressing rooms on the walls next to the doors. This time, though, they were a hard-bitten and street-wise group who had weathered the terrors of Brezhnev, Chechenya and the "Bolshoi Mac". Like Tiger John, Boris had his whole family with him – his wife, daughter and parents.

Like most circuses, the acts for this show were "bought in". Speciality acts provided their own props and music (most of which was on tape or CD of varying quality). Only in the more stylised shows like *Cirque du Soleil* was there an overall concept or artistic direction. The nearest theatrical equivalent would be Music Hall, Variety or Vaudeville.

For the first time, our tent began to look like it just might stage a show. The final preparations were being made. Ian and Al were setting the lights. With the rigging installed, the acts hastily prepared for opening night.

"No white string", Vincent's gofer moaned, returning empty handed. "Only yellow." Vincent patiently explained that yellow would be fine. The lad whom Gavin sent also returned, but without the tennis balls. "They not have them", he apologised, "so I buy three dozen sun-glasses instead." "Guanxi" in action.

Rachel, Frances and Tracy rehearsed, as Sweetpea swung aimlessly from a bungee cord, and Christina practised on the trapeze, hopeful of the day when she might do it professionally. Galena, a seventeen-year-old Russian dancer was doing her splits. Martin the Gnome whispered, "She's gonna make some man very happy some day." Lelila, from Mongolia, eighteen and exceptionally beautiful, practised with her parent's whip act. Not surprisingly, the men left her in peace.

My attention soon focused on a pony-tailed figure who seemed to be directing the proceedings. I was never formally introduced to Mike. In fact, "formality" and "Mike" probably did not exist on the same dimensional plane. He was not there when the tent was built up on the first site. Nor was he there when we tore it down and moved it. But he was here now. His intense, straight face suggested that he seldom smiled and seldom laughed because he considered it to be a waste of time. Or perhaps, in the human comedy, he just didn't get the joke. Some would call this direct approach "no nonsense", others would say it was tactless. Mike didn't care. He called the shots. He and his girlfriend Jill were now the joint Show Managers. They would finish the job that Phillip and Ian, who had gone home, had begun.

At this point, I was grateful to them, for they had brought with them three weeks worth of my mail, which I'd had forwarded to Phillip's office. This included letters from family and friends, as well as my all-important bank statements.

Mike was quickly baptised into the New Aspect way of doing things. Mr. Hsu pointed to the ring fencing and barked, "Why this there?" Mike explained that it was to keep the audience away from the animals. "But audience pay to see bear, want to see him up close. Take it away." When Yi – who was a formidable presence in her own right – objected, he sacked her. "And Hsu says he's worried about licences", Mike fumed.

After several more hours, Vincent's young lad returned once again. "How big a roll of string?" "Just get a *@#%ing roll!"

Another Taiwanese worker announced that he was shutting down the main generator. This had to be done with care, as any power surge could burn out the electrical circuits. Ian asked him to wait until he and Al were finished programming the lighting board. He said "okay!" Ian made the mistake of assuming that "okay" meant "I understand." Before Ian and Al had a chance to save their programme, the power went dead. Ian lunged at the hapless employee. If the others hadn't pulled him off, he might have killed him.

After dark, Vincent's errand boy wandered in, his shoulders slumped. "No can get string", he moaned. "Shop's closed." "What a stupid boy!" shouted Vincent. Thus, for the rest of the tour, this hapless minion would be known as Stupid-Boy. When the Lord gave out brains, this lad thought he said "drains" and pulled the plug on his.

Act I, Scene 7

"Another Openin', Another No Show"

On the eve of the opening, Jim pulled our coach up to one of Taipei's finest restaurants, and our eclectic band of Russian, Moroccan, English, Welsh, Irish, Mexican, Mongolian, American and Canadian artists and technicians trundled out, invading the top floor. The entire company was together in one place for the very first time. Clowns, acrobats, animal trainers and roustabouts encircled the tables, speaking a rich cocktail of languages.

The establishment was overwhelmed by the more than eighty members of our party. While we waited an interminable length of time for our food, the waiter plied everyone (except me, a teetotaller) with the local generically named "Taiwan Beer", of which Greg declared his intention to drink "*vast* quantities," stretching the adjective into a verbal suspension bridge.

So this time, I drank squeezed mangoes, while Greg and the others chose a stronger "jungle juice" in their quest to become bevied, dionysian, fuddled, maggoty, stotious, soaked – in other words, "pissed". After a couple of hours on an empty stomach, I would be surrounded by high spirits, if not actually in them myself.

Then came the food. For those in our party who had not given up on eating solids, the set menu, with its seafood salads, was delectable.

After two courses, I left early by taxi. We had to be up for work at seven, and I was still catching up on sleep.

Our first performance on Tuesday the twenty-eighth of October – twenty days later than originally planned – was a charity benefit. Although I didn't start work for a few hours, I decided to come in early.

Two American men turned up, hoping to find Phillip. We told them he'd gone back to England, but that Mr. Hsu was here. "Good", they said, "then he can pay us the $30,000 he owes us."

They told us about Madame Maxima, a German bear trainer with the *Great European Circus* who was stranded here with her animals for six weeks without money for food – human or otherwise – because Hsu held on to her passport.

Once again, this news did not bring me comfort. My own passport was still safe in its pouch, which I wore around my neck, clutching it every so often for reassurance.

Phillip told *China News* that rumours of a plan to sabotage the circus and set the animals free had caused them to beef up security.[13]

---

[13] *China News*, 30 October 1997.

Yi, who had been re-instated, marshalled her army of ushers like a female drill sergeant. To Arny, this was a woman after his own heart – a girl who was small (in height, if not in breadth), yet bold and commanding to the point of being fearsome. Nobody was going to pull anything over on her.

Those who wanted to see the show faced a number of obstacles. Firstly, due to our abrupt change of venue, the circus was not in the place or time that had been advertised. Then they had to find it, in an obscure industrial area. As we were soon to discover, empty lots don't have addresses.

Once they'd found us, families began turning up by the (small) carload. As the audience approached the site, they were accosted by touts selling black-market tickets for the show. Calling the police did little good – they had evidently been bribed. Then the customers passed under an exceedingly flimsy metal archway (think Buckminster Fuller as executed by a kid with a Meccano set working in the dark).

Once inside the perimeter, they would find a carnival hawking all manner of Chinese fast food. Kiosks offered cooked sausages on a stick, roasted chicken and flavoured ice called "baobing", while Kat, Alice and Marie sold popcorn and programmes. I inspected the programme, and found my name listed as "Louis Atkey". My cover was blown. Then I noticed that Greg's name had been misspelled

"Gerg". Good, I thought. If he's going to call me "Louie", I know what I can call him.

As the audience entered the tent, there was an opportunity to be kissed by a sea lion – the only kiss I would receive on the whole trip – and have their pictures taken.

Then, as the lights dimmed, the sound and fury of the circus began to take shape. Gavin picked up his microphone and growled "Ladies and Gentlemen, boys and girls, welcome to the A-MER-ican UN-i-VER-sal CIR-cus!" This was followed by an interpreter's translation, as the company paraded to the music of "Come Follow the Band" from *Barnum*. (A Broadway musical had to feature in here somewhere.) The same people who, last week, were lifting stringers and raising kingpoles were now doing acrobatics and handstands. Then Gavin introduced "Madame Kaseeva", pronouncing her name in such a way that, to Russian ears, sounded like their word for "crossed eyes".

Calling the show the *American Universal Circus* was a bit of cheek, I thought. Yes, Tiger John Campolongo and his family were from Philadelphia. And Bill and Bob, the identical twin clowns, were from Kansas City. And Chad was from Texas. But the rest were from Russia, Mongolia, Mexico, Morocco and, for the most part, England. It was a good thing acrobats didn't speak, for Tracy and Rachel's thick Mancunian accents would have given away that they were not from California. I threatened to revoke Gavin's artistic licence. "It's not artistic licence," he grunted, "It's just licence to B.S."

As the sound system blasted out a techno-pop version of "Cotton Eyed Joe", Lelila and her parents cracked their whips, while the Mexican flyers careered overhead. Then I did my bit, standing with four other crew members by the entrance to the tent, holding a rope. When our cue came, we ran with the hemp, pulling one of the flyers up into the cupola, the metal frame suspended from the roof of the tent. Nothing as sophisticated as a counter-weight fly system, but it worked.

As he gazed over the half empty house, Arny nodded. "Not bad, considering they've not had any rehearsal." Then Boris' parents came on with their performing cats and dogs, jumping through hoops. John cracked the whip over his tigers, Christina rode in gallantly on horseback and finally, I saw what the backbreaking work was really for. To the chagrin of Wu-hung's Life Conservationists, two brown bears stepped into the ring dressed in tutus and danced *Swan Lake*. Who would have thought that, in a tent in Taiwan, the performing arts would rise to such heights?

After it was over, and the "crowds" had gone, the tent was sealed up and I powered down the generators, ready for my night shift.

Entr'acte

"Le Roi du Wonton"

While Typhoon Ivan had wisely avoided us, we felt its knock-on effect, as the weather turned somewhat inclement. The word "rain" did not do it justice. The place had become "subaqueous", as though Taiwan had become Atlantis. I was in the middle of a sea of mud, and my job – all night – was to keep the water from collecting on the roof of the sea lion tent by poking it with a stick. As the rain poured down on me, I grumbled, "I'll bet Stephen Sondheim never had to do anything like this". The sea monsters may have been happy, but I wasn't.

Some of the others were having more fun. The Taiwanese version of TV's *Blind Date* was called *Extreme Man-Woman*. I could think of no more descriptive phrase for the mating ritual that had so far eluded me. Since I was out of the romantic loop, I'm not sure at what point people first began to pair up. But Paul had to call each of the guys in the morning to give them their work assignments, so he couldn't help but notice when a woman answered the phone.

Kat and Greg were the first couple to come to my attention. Gedda too had hooked up with Alice, (notwithstanding the pony-tailed figure who kissed her in a very un-brotherly fashion at Heathrow). And

Chad, a clown from Texas, had found Frances, an acrobat from Manchester. Mr. Hsu also spotted Camille, one of his Chinese employees, sitting on Chris's knee.   He muttered, "Not have enough work to do."

As for my own love dis-interest, there were certainly enough attractive women in the company. One of the Russians, a dancer from the Bolshoi, momentarily caught my eye, though I don't know if it was some remnant of the cold war, Slavic diffidence or just her poor grasp of English that blew a chilly Siberian wind in my direction. It didn't matter. A casual fling would have been anathema to me. I did not have one single frivolous bone in my body.

Since I had no other "distractions", I looked forward to experiencing Taiwanese culture away from the circus. Arny devised a schedule whereby Chris, Vaughan and I would do seven nights, seven evenings, then seven mornings in rotation. In theory, we would each have a day off every three weeks.

First, I decided to go to the cinema. In London, I usually saw several films per week, and was suffering popcorn withdrawal. In Taiwan, Hollywood films were shown in English with Chinese sub-titles. They had their own small film industry, but little of it was exported to the West, although Taiwanese-born director Ang Lee had become a major player in Hollywood. (Years earlier, I had enjoyed a Taipei-set comedy of his called *Eat, Drink, Man, Woman.*)

To begin with, I checked one of the two English newspapers – the *China News* or the *China Post* – to see when and where the film I wanted to see was playing. Buying a ticket, which cost 250 NT, was the easy part. I simply queued up at the window displaying the poster for the film I wanted to see. I hoped.

Finding the entrance was a guessing game to the Mandarin-illiterate. The box office was not even in the same building as the cinema. Then I had to find the auditorium. In this case, the auditoria were dispersed onto different floors of a department store. *Titanic* might have been playing near Men's Shoes, while *Curdled*, the film I wanted to see that night, was near Ladies Lingerie.

After using a lot of creative sign language with the staff, I found the cinema and settled down for some – popcorn? No such luck. Instead of Pic-N-Mix, there was a selection of dried fruits, seeds, or, for the addicted, "betel" nuts, which gave off a buzz comparable to injected caffeine. (The government health warnings included a picture of somebody with a disfigured mouth.) The toilets never stocked paper – you were expected to bring your own. If you were lucky, there was a Western style loo. If you were unlucky, it was a glorified hole in the floor with no seat.

The next day, I had hoped to venture further afield. The National Palace Museum, said to be one of the finest in the world, beckoned to me. It contained the treasures of the Chinese emperors spirited out (stolen?) by Chiang Kai-shek in 1949, but it was awkward to get to, especially since the roll signs on the buses were exclusively in Chinese. Instead, I settled for riding to Tanshui on the brand new and extortionately over-budget Mass Rapid Transit (MRT) system. When they were building it – according to legend – the trench they dug ran down the same road as their big annual tenth of October military parade. The steel grating over top was not strong enough to support their heavy tanks so – what did they do? Re-route the parade? Not on your life! They filled in the subway! After the parade, they dug it out again!

Tanshui ("fresh water"), a fishing village north of Taipei, was at the end of the MRT line. When I emerged from the neo-Fujian architecture of the station, I heard a small jazz band playing in the courtyard. I walked along the sea wall toward Shaluen Beach, then came across a very curious looking structure perched on the hillside.

In 1626, the Spanish conquerors from the Philippines established their first beachhead in Taiwan at Keelung. Three years later, they built their capital at Tanshui, which they called "Castillo". To defend the town, they built Fort Santo Domingo atop the hill of the "Five Tiger Height", overlooking the Tanshui River on the north and facing steep slopes on all other sides. From here, they traded with Han and the Ping-pu aborigines for deerskin and sulphur, all

the while trying to convert them to Christianity. The Dutch (or "red-haired-people" as they were locally known) had already settled on the south of the island, and were determined to keep the Spaniards in check. After a couple of failed attempts, they captured the fort and town in 1642. Thus it became known as the "castle of the red-haired-people", or Hung Mao Ch'eng. The Dutch rebuilt the fort with bricks imported from the Mainland and added cannons. In 1652, they tried to impose a poll tax, which – as any Brit will tell you – was no way to win popular support. Neither was slaughtering 6,000 peasants for that matter, so they were dispatched in 1661 by a Ming loyalist named Chang Ch'eng Kung, who had hopes to set up a shadow government in Taiwan with the aim of retaking the Mainland from the Manchus. (Does any of this sound familiar?) But in 1683 the Ch'ing dynasty of the Manchus annexed Taiwan to Fujian Province, making it officially a part of China for the first time. The fort fell into disrepair until 1724 when Emperor Yun-Cheng added an outer wall and four gates.

In 1867, after Tanshui became a free port for foreign trade, the fort was leased to the British as a Consulate, and an official residence was built nearby. It remained as such until 1972, when Britain severed diplomatic ties. After brief periods of use by Australia and the U.S., it was handed back to the Republic of China in 1980.

Walking back toward the MRT, I passed a very old temple. Lung Shuan dated from the Ch'ing dynasty, and has been designated a grade three historic site. A branch of the Lung Shuan temple in Shang-Chiang county, Fujian Province, this was built to serve the Han immigrants, and paid for by wealthy mainlanders. In its courtyard, merchants sold food, thus combining the sacred and the practical. Kuan-in, the Goddess of Mercy, is said to have helped Ch'ing soldiers to defeat the French. The Emperor then added an inscription: "Merciful Spirit Embraces Everyone".

Continuing on, I found a tiny restaurant called *"Le Roi du Won-ton"*. The walls inside were covered with Canadian pendants, newspaper clippings and travel posters. The woman who ran it had spent a few years in Montreal, and when she learned my nationality, she made a fuss, bringing me an onion cake as a special treat. Slightly refreshed, I caught the MRT back to Taipei and back to work.

Act II Scene 1

"Chinese Take-away"

Now that the show had opened, we settled down to the day-to-day business of *keeping* it open. Any visions I may have had of the "Greatest Show On Earth" were rapidly receding in my mind.

Working on the evening shift, I stood out front with Arny to maintain crowd control as the audience filed past the "condemned" sign. Due to some exciting new concepts in electrical wiring –

– Excuse me? Oh, I'm sorry. Am I getting ahead of myself? "What 'condemned' sign?" you ask. I apologise. Things like this were becoming such a common place occurrence, it was easy to forget that, to the uninitiated, they still had the power to shock.

When I arrived for work earlier in the day, the notice plastered across the entrance to our tent showed a figure of a person with a red line drawn diagonally across it. I stood there, trying to think of all the possible implications this might have. Chinese being a picture language, perhaps this was a visual pun of Hsu's name, which in impolite English circles could be taken to mean "piss off". More likely, it meant "No Human Life Forms Allowed." After a theatrical first night, actors stayed up waiting for the reviews.

Maybe in the circus, they waited to see if the authorities were going to come and kick them out.

As I stood gaping at the notice, Mr. Hsu wandered into view. I asked him about the sign, but he shrugged it off, as if it were unimportant. I persisted, and he said finally, "That just mean they say tent condemned..." Oh. Of course.

The fire chief for Taipei County, Ho Chung-fa, had declared the tent "unsafe". We were already aware that Phillip couldn't use his seats in Europe because they didn't meet safety standards: they were wooden, and had open spaces through which a match could fall. Alas, the Taiwanese authorities found even more faults. The firefighting equipment was deemed to be inadequate. Mr. Hsu was supposed to have applied to Taipei County for approval thirty days ahead of time, and they maintained he hadn't done this. Councillor Wu Shangjiu contended the circus could face fines of between 60 and 150 thousand NT per day. He added that he wished the amount could be even higher, and accused Taipei mayor (and future president) Chen Shui-bian of passing the buck.[14]. Either Taiwanese red tape had been elevated to an art form, or Mr. Hsu had enemies in high places. I tended to plunk for the latter. We may have been paying the price for that election rally. Somebody was sure getting a lot of pleasure out of this. As Taiwan's political tide was shifting, perhaps Hsu's connections no longer served him as well as they once did.

---

[14] *China News*, 30 October 1997.

As I was saying, that night I stood out front with Arny to maintain crowd control. Nobody seemed to be overly concerned about the "condemned" sign, which was there for all to see.

I was more pre-occupied with keeping the front-of-house lights working, resetting the circuit breakers every ten minutes or so. The Taiwanese electrician beamed proudly at his handiwork as Gedda asked him, "Did you go to college to learn this?" We laughed it off, comforted to know that when winter came we'd be able to warm our hands over the circuit boards.

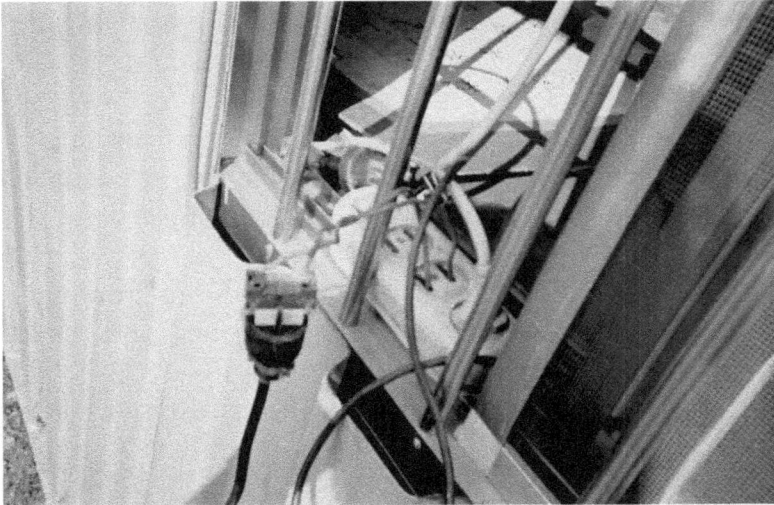

The crew were short staffed, so Paul asked me to run around back stage after the interval to help move the tigers into the tent. They were transferred out of their cages into seven wagons, or "shifting boxes". At each stage, the doors were carefully padlocked. This way, no more beasties would go walkabout into the audience in search of "Chinese take-away" as some bears had done the week before (thanks to Hsu's removal of the ring fencing). Sweetpea surreptitiously reached inside one of the cages and patted the tiger on its back. Just as well it wasn't hungry.

We ran into the tent carrying four by eight sections of a cage, which were then locked together, forming a wall around the ring. The tigers were led into this enclosure, jumping through a flaming hoop.

Then, it was the turn of the sea lions. As we pushed their shifting boxes, I counted only three animals inside. I asked about this, but was angrily told to "shush!"

After the show, Jill approached me delicately. I expected that she might have something to tell me about the missing sea lion, but I was wrong.

"We've noticed that you have a room to yourself." My shields were raised, armed and ready to do battle. "Perhaps I do", I said gingerly. "Well, everybody is meant to share." But I'm a non-smoker, I pointed out. The only one. She became aware quickly that handling feral beasts such as tigers was nothing compared to the cage she was now entering. She bravely continued. "We would like you to share with Sweetpea." The rest of our conversation was not printable.

Sweetpea, the man-child with an unruly mop of hair, was a self-described "party animal". I had no tolerance for tobacco. "Em – but I got to 'ave me fag before I go to bed," he moaned. Too bad.

Once everybody was gone, I closed up the tent, powered down the main generators and waited for the night shift to come. Around midnight, Vaughan felt his way across the site in the dark, and stumbled into the workshop. He didn't think to ask his cab to wait for me, so I went out in the street to flag one down.

I arrived at the hotel to collect my wages, only to find that there were police in Mike and Jill's room. "Sorry", said Mr. Hsu. "Mike and Jill steal your money". Yeah, right. And Mars sends ambassadors to the U.N. Besides, I knew what thieves looked like – they wore bright red polka-dotted bow ties. At least that's what Malcolm wore. He was the box office manager I'd worked with in London who absconded to New York with the proceeds of a rock concert. (He even sent us a post card.) Anyway, thinking that they might try the same sort of thing, Hsu demanded that Mike and Jill give him their passports.

As the truth began to unravel, the more learned detectives among us began to suspect that it was all a ruse. Anything that was not firmly nailed down in an ironclad contract (and backed up with the threat of military action) was subject to Hsu's whims. For example, he refused to pay Christina for her equestrian act, because she didn't have a contract. The assumption was that when he hired Tiger John, he got his whole family. John told her to stop working. Technically, without the horse, I guess we were no longer a "ma-hsi-t'uan".

In fact, we suspected that he hadn't planned to pay any of us at all, since he had apparently pulled this same stunt with the *Great European Circus* two years earlier. When Phillip got wind of this, he told Mike to pull the tent and come home.

In the end, after a lengthy stand-off, we received three-quarters of our wages, with a promise of the balance the following evening. We made it clear that if this promise were to be broken, there would be no show.

I returned to my room and found Sweetpea firmly installed there. No compromise. I literally had to step over him to use the toilet. And he snored like a hurricane. When he said he came from Wales, I didn't realise he meant the species.

Act II Scene 2
The Banker

During my interview, Louise warned me that banks in Taiwan might not be as advanced as those in England. *Not as advanced?* English banks were still in the Neolithic period, I thought. They didn't really have computers – just a little woodpecker inside the ATM scribing my receipt onto a papyrus – and they had yet to come to grips with those newfangled telephonic communicating devices. How else could you explain a four day wait to deposit a cheque? But they invariably bristled at my complaints. "Not modern? It's the most up to date in the British Empire! Why sir, your deposit was dispatched just last week by a team of the Queen's finest horses! It shall reach its destination anon!" So how bad could a Taiwanese bank be?

On top of all the other stress inducing scenarios, both real and imagined, I feared that the standing order to pay the rent on my flat in Pimlico could go sproing. I couldn't afford to have anything go wrong, so it was vitally important that my wages reached home in time.

However, whereas I had previously wired the money to my account in London, I was now wiser. Having belatedly received my statements, I saw that my bank had charged me £7 for receiving each telegraphic transfer, on top of the cost of sending it. Now I had a different plan.

Making my way upstairs to the foreign exchange department of Hua Nan Commercial Bank, I found a young woman with a working knowledge of English. I explained that I wanted to buy a banker's draft in Sterling, and handed over 10,000 NT in cash. Then she went to a computer to calculate the exchange rate, deducting a service charge of about 350 NT.

Once I'd received the draft, I then made my way to a post office. Unlike the bank, where they were accustomed to dealing with foreigners, it was a challenge to find anyone with even a smattering of English. I was able to make them understand that I wanted to send it Registered Mail, which cost me about 100 NT. Although slower, this was significantly cheaper than a telegraphic transfer.

Now I'd become known as the "Banker", and other members of the company came to me for advice on how to send their money home.

In her eagerness to sign me on board, Louise assured me that New Aspect was solid like a rock. Having learned that this "rock" was somewhat porous – possibly even volcanic – I was very glad that I had arranged that overdraft facility. Nefarious characters arrived each night to nab the box office receipts. It was beginning to occur to us that our problems in getting paid were due to something more serious than Hsu's staff not getting to the bank in time.

The more I learned about New Aspect's financial situation, the more discomfited I was. A few months earlier, Mr. Hsu had attempted to bring the *"Three Tenors"* (Luciano Pavarotti, Placido Domingo and José Carreras) to Taipei. Their agent, Matthias Hoffman, entered into negotiations, but later withdrew. This resulted in his being sued by New Aspect for breach of contract. A New York district court threw the suit out, saying that no contract existed because payment terms had not been finalised, the defendants believing that New Aspect "intended to default"[15]. The *"Super Concert of the Century"* ultimately went ahead under the stars on the grounds of the Chiang Kai-shek Memorial, with Dianna Ross (!) standing in for Pavarotti. Although it was packed out with 60,000 people watching, only about a quarter of them had actually bought tickets. According to Yi, security was so poor it lost something like $4,000,000 U.S. This debt had badly crippled New Aspect, nearly bankrupting the company[16], forcing Hsu to sell some of his homes. (None of this would put Domingo off from working with New Aspect again: he returned for another concert in 2007.) They attempted, with little success,

---

[15] Supreme Court, New York County, Index No. 104097/97, P.C. No. 12934, *New Aspect Promotion Corporation and International New Aspect Cultural and Educational Foundation, plaintiffs, against Hoffman Concerts, Inc., Hoffman Konzerte GmbH and Matthias Hoffman, Defendants.*
[16] "Hsu is a Cultural Warrior", *Taipei Times*, 13 November 2005

to sell off the leftover merchandise in our front of house.

The impact of the company's disarray showed in a number of ways. Mr. Hsu had struck a deal for the use of our site, which belonged to our friendly neighbourhood municipal candidate. This involved allowing him to use our tent for an election rally. Political dissent had been suppressed for so long that it now bubbled like freshly opened champagne, opinions supported by fists. This rally was to be no exception.

Hsu's other "solution" was to begin sacking people, starting with Jill, Rachel, Frances, Tracie, Kat, Alice and Marie, allegedly because they didn't smile enough. The smiles quickly returned to their faces when they heard that Phillip was on his way with a solicitor. Frances got sick of being fired and quit, to the disappointment of Chad, her boyfriend. A few more were tempted to follow her, but I was determined not to become cynical. Wait and see.

Act II Scene 3
Week Four
"TONIGHT'S WORD IS SUICIDE"

I thought I'd lucked out when the taxi driver spoke perfect English. Then I handed him the address, and he shook his head. "Sorry", he said. "I don't read Chinese". (He was Malaysian.)

The routine of keeping the show running also meant trying to stay centred while everything around us resembled a whirling dervish. On the other hand, if I wanted to lose myself, this would be easily accomplished.

As I arrived on site for the night shift, Boris was getting ready to leave. Earlier, he had seen some people throwing rocks over the fence at the animals, and told me, "I bringing killer dog from Russia. He good guard dog." The sea lion compound was barricaded, and nobody but the handlers were allowed near.

I asked him, "What happened to the fourth sea lion?" He was initially evasive, but finally allowed that it was "probably a heart attack." Ironically, Boris believed that, because of the animal rights protesters, the animals were held too long in quarantine and suffered for it.

My own involvement in animal welfare was restricted to guarding them at night. Like Paul said, counting the tigers. The animal trainers seemed like nice people, and they were my friends – at least for the duration of this tour.

I began to settle into what would become my routine. Now I was alone in the workshop, with only the beasties – and mosquitoes – to keep me company. Although it was mid-November, it was hot and humid, and I had no protection against insects.

The Chihuahuas yapped as soon as anybody came near, so I began to play a game to amuse myself. I crept up on them. Next, I began to bark, setting off a chorus of replies.

Then, from out of the dark, I heard the most ghastly sound. One of the tigers was moaning and bashing himself against the sides of his cage. He's hungry, I thought, and knows I would do just nicely. Concerned, I called John. "Nothing to worry about", he said. "He's just horny." Just what I needed, another lonely heart. I comforted myself dreaming of all the damage I could do if I had his teeth and claws. I steered clear of the bears, though. Standing in their cages, rocking back and forth and staring straight ahead, they resembled Travis Bickle with fur.

When I grew tired of barking at dogs, I turned on the radio. Taiwan had an English language radio station called International Community Radio Taipei which played a wide range of music. Even out there, I could listen to a tribute to Jerome Kern, or to the

BBC World Service. Radio Canada International was available on short wave.

I heard on the news that our candidate in Taipei had lost the election. Good. In fact, Taiwan's young democracy had just received a seismic jolt. The ruling Kuomintang (nationalist) party was routed for the first time in history. The opposition Democratic Progressive Party took eight out of fifteen local county councils. For much of the country, it was the first time that anybody but the KMT had ever been in power, and seemed to signify the genesis of the greater changes to come. Hsu was very publicly identified with the KMT. Oh dear.

I spun the dial looking for anything else interesting, and found a Chinese station giving English lessons. An American sounding voice said cheerfully, "Good evening class: Tonight's word is *suicide*". I sat and listened, transfixed, as they illustrated the uses of this word with examples. "Kevin was very depressed..." I imagined some poor git hanging on by a thread, writing a letter to his English lover, and the only thing keeping him alive was his limited vocabulary.

As I sat in the workshop, I was gradually devoured by a swarm of mosquitoes who no doubt mistook my pink complexion for rare meat.

In the morning, as I stumbled to 7Eleven for my dose of "Calcium Drink", the passers-by screamed in horror at my swollen, misshapen face. With one eye almost shut, I must have resembled the Elephant Man.

Crawling up the road to a pharmacist, I managed to spit out the words "Bug repellent". "Wei?"[17] asked the uncomprehending shop clerk. "Bug" I said, pointing to my raging pustule of a face. "Repellent!" (A word which in my present condition called for very little talent at Charades.) Unable to understand me, she simply moved on to the next customer.

I lurched, Quazimodo style, into the next pharmacist, pointing to the shelf behind the counter.

"Bug!" I exclaimed excitedly. The chemist put his hand to a bottle on the shelf. I shook my head, and shouted "Bug!" again. He moved his hand up to the next shelf. "Bug!" He advanced up another tier,

---

[17] Mandarin for *"huh?"*

as I waived my arms. "Repellent!" He moved his hand to the right. "Repellent!" He moved over to the next product. "Yes!" I shouted joyously. "Hse-hse!"

Act II Scene 4
"Home Sweet Whorehouse"

Week Five

There was a point beyond the frying pan and the fire, and we'd reached it. Yeah, this was it. The moment of truth. When we finished in Taipei, the news came down that in the next city, we were expected to share not only rooms, but also beds. "I ain't never shared no bed with no bloke", Arny hollered, "and I'll be damned if I'll do it for Hsu." We can pack it in and go home.

But wait a minute. Home to what? I didn't have a job to go back to. I was broke. They had us up against a wall. Between a rock and a hard place and all that. We were not exactly in a strong bargaining position. Or maybe we were. The Taiwanese didn't know anything about putting on a circus (although one local man tried to pass himself off to another company as an expert after spending an afternoon watching us raise the tent.)

But there was another reason for me to stay. I didn't yet have that certain "je ne sais quoi" that I came for. And what was that? I wanted to face a challenge, and stick it out.

Eventually, one of Hsu's minions arrived with a signed memorandum pledging us individual beds.

We were appeased. For now. And so the demolition began.

Then Greg let out a yell – he had pulled a muscle in his back. Our first casualty – and he was at least a decade younger than me.

"Don't lift it like that", Chris told me, as I tried to hoist a stringer. "You'll put your back out." "My back is already out," I yelled. He demonstrated: "Kneel down, and lift from the base of your spine." Yeah, yeah, I knew all that. Trouble was, I was forty, not twenty. My joints were so stiff I couldn't kneel.

Once the tent was down, the order was given that it was not to leave Taipei until Phillip had been paid for the hire.

I "chipped in and helped out" from 9:30 Sunday night until 11:00 Monday morning, when we were sent back to our hotel for a rest, to return by 2:00. If that wasn't bad enough, for this brief respite we were required to move hotels. Fresh and rejuvenated after a good twenty minutes' sleep, I resumed the task of throwing heavy things around with alacrity.

As afternoon blurred into evening, and my heart pounded with adrenaline, I had a narrow brush with death. Our portable toilets, (or as the English called them, "bogs") were locked, so I stepped between two containers to "use the facilities". It was dark, and I didn't know that a crane was lifting one of them. Only a loud yell saved me from a crushed skull.

We were so weary and famished that we began to slow down. I sorted through the old, rotten, splintered pallets, looking for any that might be salvageable. After the tent was dropped and the kingpoles lowered, all that remained for us to do was to pick up the stakes and other small items, yet that took several hours. At one juncture, Paul and I went in to one of the containers out of sight to take a break. Every once in a while, Paul would pick up an "A frame" and drop it, so that it sounded like we were busy. We slogged it out until about 11:00 at night.

Then we sat on the bus while Mike hunted for a place for us to stay. About 1:30 AM, we retired to the Kindly Hotel across the street. Again we were asked to share beds, but everyone declined. The scenario and decor were familiar: round bed, mirrors on the ceiling, the works. Home sweet whorehouse.

In my dream (hallucination?) that night, Hsu, ever anxious to save money, had found a way to recycle those rotten pallets – they were used to make cages for the beasties. Every time they rubbed the sides, they would knock out one of the planks, and I would have to nail it back on before they escaped, watching out for their claws.

The following morning, we rolled out of bed, and, Phillip having been paid, packed the tent onto the trailer. Fiona, Mr. Hsu's assistant, contended that all those straps were surely unnecessary to secure the load. She complained, with no sense of irony, that Mike was incompetent. He erupted, and gave Hsu an ultimatum: it's her or him. Mike lost. He knew his business, but he was no diplomat. On to Taichung and our next brothel.

Act III, Scene 1
Like Water for Petrol

"On the road again..." Finally we were out of Taipei, and beginning our tour. Due to the delays in Taipei, our booking in Hsin Chu, where we should have opened on 8 November, was cancelled, and we went straight on to Taichung.

Our bus journey was an eerie cocktail of the familiar and the exotic. Trundling down the freeway in the dark with smiling Jim at the wheel, we passed highway signs with their customary reflective white on green lettering, but with Chinese characters as well as English, and "men at work" pictograms that showed labourers in pointed bamboo hats. We paused at a rest stop, "de-hungering" ourselves at Macdonald's.

"I'll have a Big Mac with no cheese and a large Coke, please." The attendant smiled eagerly. "Big Mac, no cheese, *flies*, Coke." No fries, I said emphatically. "No flies". Pause for effect, then: "Ketchup?" I smouldered, "And just what would I be putting ketchup on?" He shrank away timidly, then cheerfully delivered my order: Big Mac with no cheese, large Coke and *fries*.

As we continued on our journey, we began plastering tattoos of spacemen on each other's faces.

As the coach entered the city, the main strip we drove down was ignited by garish neon signs advertising video karaoke bars, or "KTV"s, resembling some sort of "Las Vegas on the China Sea". We pulled in to the Hsi Cia Mei Hotel, and thirty-five little green men, all trying to look deadly serious, trundled out, ready to confront Mr. Hsu.

"We should demand to be allowed at least eight hours' sleep before we start work", Paul suggested. "Can everyone please meet up here in the hotel foyer in half an hour?"

Arny, who had been imbibing heavily, disagreed. "We don't have a manager. Nobody can tell us to do anything." Only a cocktail of fatigue and alcohol could have turned this into an argument.

Then the rooms were allocated. I was meant to be paired with Mieczyslaw[18] our tent master. A Pole, he spoke some German, but no English. One of the Moroccans also knew some German, but again no English. Evidently Mieczyslaw was hired on somebody's recommendation, and Phillip never thought to raise the question of language. (I can only guess that his interview was even less enlightening than mine was.) So, he thought in Polish, translated into German then proceeded linguistically across Eastern Europe and down the coast of North Africa before reaching our ears and brains. In any case, I was excused by an error: Mieczyslaw was on the accommodation list twice – once under his first name,

---

[18] Pronounced "Met-tok".

once under his surname. And since few people could spell or pronounce either one of them, so far, the error had not been discovered by anybody who cared.

Around five o'clock in the morning, my much overdue slumber was broken off by a phone call. It was Arny belching out something to the effect of "be on the site by eight". I spent the next two hours stewing – "Why couldn't he have waited until seven to tell me that?"

The site was just a five-minute walk from the hotel. At least I wouldn't run up any more cab bills. I turned up for work at eight, but it didn't last long. Arny put me back on night security, so I was once again spared the drudgery. With the afternoon free, I set out to explore my environs.

My mother, who with my father had travelled to Mainland China, thought that I would find Taiwan fascinating because "China is so old". In truth, the oldest thing there was me. Most buildings looked as if they'd been constructed within the last fifteen years.

Taichung was a cultural and educational centre. It was much cleaner than Taipei – but then, so were most places.

So far, I'd had no success with finding souvenirs to send home to my family. Nary a post card was to be had. An engraved teaspoon for my mother seemed too much to ask – so much for "all the tea in China". But I was determined to find something, and it had damn well better say "Made in Taiwan" on the label. The Taiwan Museum of Art, opened in 1988 by the Taiwan Provincial government, sounded like a good place to start. A modern rectangular building, it stood three stories high, with exterior walls decorated in natural slate. Its 30,799 square metres housed an impressive collection of watercolours and calligraphy by Taiwanese artists. I couldn't get much more unique than that, so I bought an imprinted tee shirt.

As I passed a school, I paused to look at the children in the yard. They all stopped to look back at me. Having white skin was like having a twenty-four hour follow spot shining on me. "Ha-RO!" they shouted, almost in unison. I was a curiosity. "Why your face have hair on it?"

Continuing into the older part of Taichung, I passed a political demonstration of some sort. They were banging on gongs, setting off firecrackers and carrying banners, in English, proclaiming the "Republic of Taiwan", a motto of the independence-minded Democratic Progressive Party.

The Chinese love affair with noise was legendary[19]. At the height of the Cold War, Chiang Kai-shek built the world's biggest loudspeaker on the island of Kinmen three miles from the mainland in order to bombard them with beatitudes to capitalism. The Mainland Chinese built an equally bombastic contraption on their side. The din was stupendous. Eventually, they arrived at an unspoken arrangement whereby one party would blast their cacophony on Mondays, Wednesdays and Fridays, while the other took responsibility for Tuesdays, Thursdays and Saturdays. I don't know what they did about

---

[19] An anthology of Taiwanese poetry, published by Columbia University in 1987, was called *Isle Full of Noises*.

Sundays, but I'm sure they found some way to fill the void.

As I approached the railway station, the buildings became older and more rundown. The station itself looked like it dated from the Japanese occupation, but the rolling stock was all very modern. The Taiwan Railway Administration had spent a great deal of money on electrifying their main line, and buying a fleet of brand new Korean and Japanese-built passenger trains. (There were greater plans afoot: a decade later, a high speed line would connect Taipei to Kaohsiung.)

Near the station, I met a young Englishman who was my exact counterpart. He had first immigrated to Vancouver, where he directed industrial videos. Now he was teaching English here. I told him about some of our experiences. I had come expecting that the Taiwanese would put us to shame. He shook his head. "You're thinking of Japan."

I passed a number of motor-scooters with faux-English slogans emblazoned on their seats. *"We Reach for the Sky: Neither Does Civilisation"*. *"Movie: New Concepts By My Own"*.

When I returned to the hotel, I examined the label on the tee shirt I'd bought, and found the legend "Myself Studio" embroidered on top of – yes – a Canadian flag.

Before starting work, I joined the crew for a meal at a pub called *"Teh Pig and Whistle"*. This "English" pub, located in a leisure complex behind our site, resembled some sort of grotesque *Star Trek* holodeck simulation. I wondered what *"Teh"* meant. Was it Chinese? Was it ancient Saxon? Then it hit me: they had actually mis-spelled *"The"*. "That's because they're id*o*its", said Greg.

We knew that Hsu was looking for somebody to sack. He'd already tried the Russian dancers, but he lost that battle when all their comrades went out on strike. Next, he focused his attention on the English popcorn sellers, terminating Kat and Alice yet again. This time he meant business. I said to Greg and Gedda, their boy friends, "Are we going to sit still for this?" They were frustrated because they felt they were in conflict of interests, but I thought that if he could break their contracts, he could break anybody's. "Thanks, Louie." We all shook hands in agreement.

When I returned to work, I couldn't find the small generator I needed for power. No generator, no word processor, and thus these pages would be blank. At last I pinpointed it running outside one of the containers. As I drew closer, I found about thirty people crammed inside. The Russians were having a birthday party for Boris' daughter Natasha, who had just turned thirteen. There was oodles of Russian food and much vodka flowing. Gavin was swivelling about like a joystick.

The last of the revellers staggered back to their hotel about half past two. I moved the generator back and filled the tank, but couldn't start it. I checked the oil and it was fine. I spent the night in darkness, without a radio. Only the grunts of the tigers broke the silence.

I settled down for the night in my steel packing crate. A Chinese guard came in and lit a stick of incense, meant to keep the mosquitoes away. Next to the burning incense was a five-gallon petrol container.

In the dark, a bevy of highly intoxicated Taiwanese welders were fashioning something mysterious. As their torches flashed and sparkled, I wondered – what could it be? A gallows? A Trojan panda? They worked into the night. When I say "worked", I mean they laughed, they drank, they chewed betel nuts, while sparks lit up the sky and metal rods careened wildly about. These same welders had built the arch that lurched and swayed over our entrance.

It emerged that their latest project had something to do with the two skateboarders, Pete from England and Joki[20] from Sweden, who had been hired sight unseen on the pretext that a lot of money had been spent on building this ramp. They got here and found that no such ramp had been built, and so they wound up sitting on their duffs and not getting paid. Finally, a structure was taking shape. And what a shape it was. When it was finished, there was just one problem: it was too big for the ring.

Then as the rising sun glistened against the rusty containers, and all things invisible became visible again, I realised to my horror the mistake I had

---

made. The latest delivery of drinking water came in containers virtually identical to the petrol cans. Since I couldn't read Chinese, it was pretty hard to tell the difference in the dark and with no warning. Gedda bled the fuel lines, heated the spark plugs and eventually got it running. "If it had worked, Mel" declared Paul, "you'd be a rich man."

Mike was soon re-instated as show manager. We were relieved to have somebody competent in charge, although some feared he may have compromised himself to death, and that he was no longer on our side. "To be fair", said Paul, "He's trying to do a job that doesn't want to be done."

On the first night, 21 November 1997, the show was an hour late going up because the crane deposited the generator too far away from the tent, and the cord didn't reach. (I'm not making any of this up.) Paul turned to our portly house manager and said "Yi, give us a song." "Why?", she asked wearily. "Then it'll be over, and we can all go home."

Act III, Scene 2

"BULLETS ARE EXPENSIVE"

Week Six

I arrived by taxi at eight in the morning to find the workshop container sealed up. As I cracked open the door, my bleary eyed colleague from the night shift emerged yawning and stretching, wearing pyjamas, slippers, a robe and a night-cap with a pipe dangling from his mouth. (Okay, I'm exaggerating slightly.) Once he set out for the hotel (and yet more rest), I lifted up the wallings on the tent in order to air it out.

Then the day crew arrived on the bus. Simon wasn't with them. Nobody knew where he was – he just didn't turn up. Paul, who was now "Tent Foreman", exploded into an impression of King Kong, scattering seating boards and shouting a plethora of obscenities. After this brief catharsis, he calmed down and became his affable self again, and we set to work.

Short-handed as we were, Paul told me that I was under no obligation to help them. It was not, strictly speaking, a part of my job, although there was no way I was going to sit around and watch everybody else do all the work.

The first order of the day was rubbish pick-up. That meant raking up the food and drink and other unmentionables that had been slung under the seats. Boiled chicken feet were disgusting enough when fresh, never mind in their half eaten, discarded form. I had to climb under the seating from behind, stooping over. My back did not stoop very easily, and six weeks of heavy lifting hadn't improved matters.

As I did this, I heard a growling sound behind me that sent shivers down my vertebral column. All my experience of camping in the Canadian Rockies had taught me to be terrified whenever I heard bears, especially when I was covered in rubbish, but it was only the Russians rehearsing the cub. Then I saw something that broke my heart.

Up until this point, I had seen the animals in their cages, being fed, being transported and performing. I had not seen them being trained. Then I heard the baby bear hollering, peeing on the ground in fear as his Russian handlers slapped and kicked him to get him to do what they wanted.

With all the attention being given to us by animal welfare activists, surely, I thought, they would avoid such flagrant abuses. I didn't know what to think. I wasn't sure if this little bear would be better off in the wild, but I was pretty sure he'd be happier if somebody wasn't putting a boot to his backside. Was this really necessary? So far, I'd seen little evidence of cruelty to the tigers. (Who would dare?) The sea lions – those who were still alive – seemed all right. But it was plain to see that the bears wore deep psychological scars. According to People for the Ethical Treatment of Animals, muzzling a bear can interfere with its vision and breathing.

John could not understand the accusations of animal cruelty. He maintained that he treated his animals like they were his children. But getting food for his "cats" was a struggle: at one point, Hsu suggested that they could eat frozen chicken.

With the exception of whips and muzzles, I did not see any implements used. Unlike some circuses, there were no cattle prods. But nor did they have much room for exercise. PETA describes swaying back and forth, head bobbing and pacing as symptoms of mental distress. The tigers paced, and the bears did all three.

Still, I had a job to do. Whatever pangs my conscience might have been feeling, I was under contract in a foreign country, and my options were severely limited. I realised that the only way I could do any good was to stay and write about it.

The show was growing and evolving. Acts were being cut and new ones added. We were finally getting around to putting in the motorcycle trapeze act, in which Mounir, one of the Moroccan tumblers, balanced a motorcycle on the tightrope, with Tracy and Rachel, the acrobats, dangling below. (Mounir couldn't ride a bike on solid ground, but that didn't seem to bother anyone.) Like the skateboard ramp, this prop was never properly designed, only this time it was an English error. The bike, donated as part of a sponsorship deal by Yamaha, did not have the same brakes as the special wheel that Phillip sent from England, which had a groove cut in the tires.

The welders cut away at the bike, with sparks flying inches away from the (full) petrol tank. Knowing I was very safety conscious, Paul advised "You might want to avert your eyes."

The props were rebuilt, and we were off and running. Or not. The tension on the base plate was pulling the stakes out of the ground, and it all collapsed. The hell with it. This particular flying act would never get off the ground.

Never mind. Carry on. Hsu wanted us to smarten up our containers, so we asked Vincent for ten cans of blue paint. We waited. We waited some more. Then we broke for lunch.

On our way to the restaurant, Greg tempted fate by asking, "Do you suppose Simon's been abducted by aliens?" At that moment, we came to an intersection where a lobster, recently escaped from a seafood restaurant, was waiting for the traffic light to change so that it could cross the street. "Gerg", I said, "We've *all* been abducted by aliens".

The tiny restaurant down the street served us all we could eat and drink for 100 NT, or about £2. Our steaks, rice, cabbage and onions were fried on the counter right in front of us. We used our chopsticks to eat them fresh from the grill.

As I watched the chefs bantering among themselves, clutching their meat cleavers, I said to Greg "I think Mandarin makes a good fighting language, don't you? For all we know, they may be talking about the weather. Whereas with, say, Swedish, they would maintain their neutrality and give each other the Nobel Peace Prize." "That's true, Louie", he nodded, "but nothing can beat *Klingon*."

I asked Paul, how did this show stack up in his experience? "So – so", he grunted. "My favourite was a small family circus in Ireland. It was more friendly." He wasn't a fan of shows like *Cirque du*

Soleil, though. "Too highbrow", he said. "Takes the fun out of it."

I told him about what I'd seen the Russians do to the little bear. "Yeah," he sighed, "I have to look away when they do that." Russian circuses had always had a harsh reputation. But then, he pointed out, if they banned animal circuses, the bears would have to be put down.

When we returned, there was still no paint. "It has to go through the f***ing idiocracy first" said Greg, so we went on to our next task, to wash the foyer tent. We laid it out on the ground, then scrubbed it with soap and water, using brooms. To dry, we sprinkled sawdust, then swept it away.

At the end of the shift, Vincent finally arrived – with only five cans of paint, waiting for which we'd lost a days' work.

Simon eventually wandered in, offering Paul some well thought out excuse. Paul stared at him long and hard, but said nothing.

For some reason, Simon chose later to reveal to me the real reason for his absence: "If you awoke with a beautiful woman lying next to you," he suggested, "would you want to leave her to pick up rubbish in a tent?" I hadn't realised they gave work visas to extraterrestrials. *You picked the wrong guy to tell that sob story to, mate.* Call me a prude, call me unsympathetic, but if I was going to have to live like a monk, so should the rest of the world. If Mike had his way (and on this rare occasion, he did) Simon would soon be on a plane back to Blighty. The poor lad thought we would band together for him in the same way we had for Kat and Alice. He was wrong.

That night, there was a party in one of the hotel rooms. Arny sat slouched in an easy chair, his eyes bloodshot from a profuse intake of Taiwan Beer, muttering about his impending departure. "I phoned the wife", he drawled. "Luv, I'll be home for Christmas." He repeated this over and over, as if he'd forgotten that he'd already announced it several times. But when Vaughan turned up, he snarled, "You're supposed to be at work." Vaughan laughed. He said it again, "Get to work!" Vaughan laughed again. Oblivious to the incongruity, Arny ordered

Vaughan back to work while simultaneously reminding us of his own desertion plans.

That night I dreamed that the Chinese Triads were shooting at us. Paul the diplomat said, "Right, we're not having it. Nobody is doing any more work 'til you lot stop this." When we finally realised that they were only shooting at Simon, we reached for our wallets and said, "Look, we appreciate that bullets must be expensive..."

Act III, Scene 3

THE CASANOVA FROM CASABLANCA

Week Seven

As I walked the two blocks from the hotel to the circus, I found Mr. Hsu sitting by himself in a street side cafe, his head buried in his hands. As threatened, Arny had fled the coop, accompanied by Robbie, the forklift driver. This left Hsu very perplexed. Hsu's version: "They seemed happy". Arnie's version: "He's f***ing mental".

I was tempted to say something, but I thought better of it. Yet, I almost felt sorry for him. It seemed as though he were coming unglued. Were we barking up the wrong tree? To our way of thinking, Mr. Hsu might have been a few chops short of a stick, but it seems that he found us to be equally puzzling. He later told the *China News*, "It's so difficult to run a circus. You know, the circus people are not as educated. They're like hoboes. You have to talk to them in a different way. Sometimes you have to explain something five times or ten times. But then, when you open your eyes, there's another problem... When they quarrel and hate each other, and when they do stupid things, I have to solve it. I ask them not to hurt each other."[21]

Surely there must be a way to make sense out of everything. I used to think that insecure people were like wounded deer. Now I know that they are more like wounded bears: when cornered, they could become treacherous. "It certainly has been a learning curve", admitted Mike (with phenomenal understatement).

Then Hsu tried to flex what muscles he had left by firing Kat and Alice again. My conciliatory stance was put on hold, and we switched into "bolshie" mode. The thought of bringing things to a standstill got our adrenaline pumping. This was a test. He might decide to sack the lot of us and try to get by with a Chinese crew. The same solicitor who was representing Pete and Joki thought the girls had a good case.

Jill said, "Don't take any action unless you know you've got all the artists behind you." I felt sure that I could count on Boris' support. He had given me a great "All for one, one for all" sort of speech that

---

[21] *China News*, 5 April 1998.

he probably learned in his Young Communist League days, but the others took this with a pinch of salt. "What about going to the press?" But Jill sensed, "Hsu thinks he's immune to bad publicity."

"What about the sea lion?" I inquired.

The blood drained from Jill's face as her rage mounted. She mistakenly believed this to be a closely guarded secret.

It was true that if the animal rights activists got wind of the sea lion death, it would be game over. I thought surely we had Hsu by the short and curlies with this, but there was a problem. Boris faced possible arrest if he returned to Russia without the death certificate, which Hsu had so far refused to turn over. The Russian agriculture ministry would need proof that he had not sold the animal.

Although many of us were prepared to put our jobs on the line, we were far from united. There was much distrust, not all of it deserved. Yi, whom Hsu had re-instated as the house manager, was the only Taiwanese staff member with prior circus experience. She was also related to Hsu. To Yi, this was her cross to bear. To some others, it made her a snake in the grass. She knew only too well how incompetent her colleagues were, but there was nothing she could do about it. She just heaved a heavy sigh and tried to get on with it.

Greg had given his notice, due to his back injury. And, he added, "I'm just not having fun." I asked "What about Kat?" "Oh, that's not serious. That's just a frolic while we're here." Uh-huh.

Many of the Taiwanese wanted to mix with our "tribe", and I think they felt genuinely hurt when they found they weren't trusted. Not that this multicultural cross-pollination was in any way encouraged (or even tolerated) by Hsu, as Chris and Camille knew all too well.

Erica's sniffing finally uncovered the hotel error made in my favour, and I was forced to share again. Mieczyslaw was contractually guaranteed a single room. Mounir, the only other non-smoker, was a Muslim who had to get up several times in the night to pray to Mecca. Sacha, the musician, was unhappy with his own arrangements, but wouldn't share with a non-Russian. Once again, I came back to my room to find Sweetpea on the phone, organising his social life. I tried to sleep as he yacked for over an hour. Then, he turned the light out, pushed the starter button, turned up the throttle and "z-z-z-Z-Z-Z-zzz".

It wasn't just the noise that bothered me. My space was being violated. Accustomed to being on my own, I resented having to accommodate someone else. It began to occur to me that it might have been just as well that Cynthia had ik-snayed my advances, since this misanthropic outlook – coupled with a laissez-faire approach to housekeeping – might have militated against marital bliss.

Some form of rest and relaxation had now moved up several places on my list of priorities. I hadn't had a day off in over a month, and I didn't come seven thousand miles just to sit inside a shipping container listening to the grunts and farts of some transvestite plantigrades.

Then I heard that Ken had organised a coach trip to his hometown in the mountains at Sun Moon Lake. Although I was supposed to be back at work by four, I asked if somebody could cover me. Chris said, "Just go. There's enough Taiwanese security here." I knew others took "days off" this way, but I wasn't satisfied with that. "It's your judgement call", said Paul. I asked Boris, and he felt there'd be enough animal handlers on site that I could afford to be a couple of hours late. Or to be more frank, I had passed the point of caring what Ken, Vincent or Mr. Hsu thought.

Besides, we now had Ludwig, Boris' "killer dog", the biggest wuss on four legs. The worst that could happen would be that he might slobber you to death. That is, if you were of European extraction. Being by definition a "son-of-a-bitch", he had an instinctive dislike for the Taiwanese, and wouldn't let any of them anywhere near the compound.

So, on the morning of our show's first dark Monday, Vaughan and I joined the artists on the bus, while the crew stayed behind to work. As if to punish us for skiving off, the bus broke down en route, and ground to a halt near a small shop.

"Hey, look at this!" Vaughan shouted, holding

up a bottle. On closer inspection, I could see that it was filled with fermented bees. "Killer Bee Wine", said the label. "I bet it has quite a sting", he quipped. And what are you meant to do with it? The answer did not bear contemplating. Vaughan plunked down his money. He later claimed to have drunk it, although nobody believed him.

I considered buying a pointed bamboo hat like the workers in the rice patties wore, but didn't know how I'd pack it. "So what?" slurred Gavin. "You're never getting out of here alive, anyway!"

Professor Lu, a friend of Mr. Hsu's and an expert in Slavic studies, was our interpreter. Hsu had brought him on board to deal with the Russians, exciting fears that he might be trying to make us redundant. Already some of the crew felt that Professor Lu was delivering his translated orders as if he were giving them himself.

As I stood in the late November air, wearing only a tee shirt, Professor Lu asked, "How do you like Taiwanese winter?" If this was winter, then I liked it a lot.

Our bus fixed, we continued on to Sun-Moon (rì-yuè-tán), Taiwan's biggest natural lake. Situated roughly in the centre of the island, with Nenggao Mountain to the north and Yushan Mountain to the south, it is filled by water from Yushan and Alishan streams. The lake is bisected by a small islet – to the south-west the lake is crescent shaped, while to the north-east it is round: hence the name Sun-Moon. The surface of the water is 760 metres above sea-level. It is twenty-seven metres deep, its perimiter 35 km and the surface area 900 hectares.

Professor Lu explained that there were a number of legends regarding the origins of Sun Moon Lake. According to one, the native aboriginal Thao people were working in the fields when they heard a

loud noise. They looked up and saw that the sun and moon had disappeared. After several days of darkness, a brave couple ventured up into the mountains in search of them. Looking down, they saw that two dragons were holding the sun and moon captive. The couple slew the dragons using a golden axe, and restored the sun and moon to their rightful places in the sky. The holes left in the ground where they had lain filled with water, and became Sun Moon Lake.

Another legend claims that a group of hunters were chasing a white deer through the forest. They followed it for three days until it disappeared. Then they came to the lake, and finding the soil around it to be fertile, they made their homes there. They called the lake Shui Shalian – the Long Lake, or "where water and sand meet".

Europeans used to call it Lake Candidius after a 17th century Dutch Missionary named Georgius Candidius. The "sun" and "moon" sections of the lake are separated by a small island called Lalu, which was the traditional home of the Thao tribe. In 1934 the Japanese built a power plant that changed the depth of the lake from 6 metres to 27 metres. As a result, the Thao were forcibly removed from their homes. When Chiang Kai-shek retook Taiwan, he renamed the island Kuang Hua (meaning Chinese brilliance) and a wedding pavillion was built there in 1978. Since then, out of deference to the Thao people, who still consider Lalu to be a sacred place, it has reverted to its original name, and is now off limits to visitors. The Thao people now run an aboriginal cultural centre near the lake, which is open to the public. (Sadly, we didn't get to it.)

Our first stop was Wenwu, the temple of the scholar and the warrior. Built in 1938, it replaced two earlier temples that were destroyed when the power plant was built. In front of the temple was a large and ornate arch, framing a spectacular vista of the lake below. Professor Lu explained how it commemorated

Confucius and Guan Yu, a famous Han general. Another temple nearby honoured the monk who brought Buddhism to China from India.

Now I saw how circus people behaved on holiday. The Russians were in swimming, while the Moroccan tumblers formed a pyramid and dove from the pier. The show-offs. There was a reason for this display of manliness and testosterone: Mounir was spending a lot of time with Galena, who in turn was on auto-flirt. I was told that, "If it's female and breathes, the Casanova from Casablanca will be straight in there."

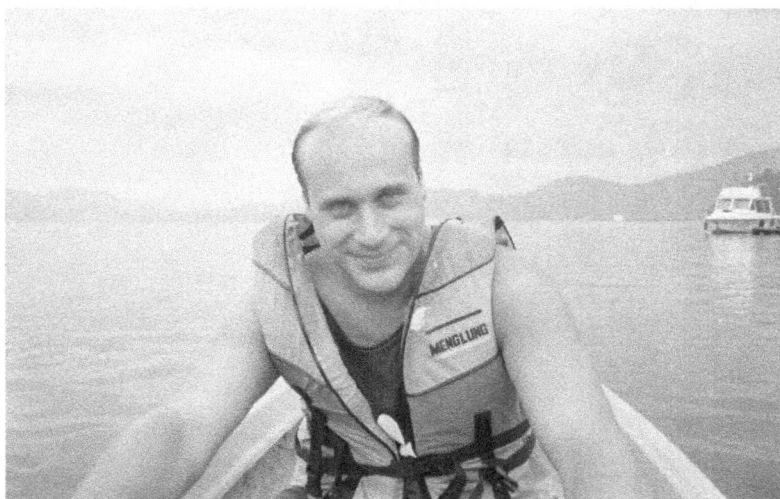

Vaughan and I rented a rowboat. I managed to persuade him to do all the rowing. I was glad it didn't tip over, as the lake was said to be full of piranhas, and the idea of my toes being used to pick some fish's teeth held little appeal for me.

On the pier, there was a wedding going on. We were in the Gretna Green of Taiwan. When Vaughan asked the groom if he could have his picture taken with the bride, I hid.

I arrived back at the site about seven. It was deserted, with no one covering me. I went through my check list. Tigers? "Roar". Bears? "Growl". Sea Lions? "Splash." Horses? "Neigh". Geese? "Honk". Ludwig? "Woof". All present and accounted for.

Act IV, Scene 1
"Tentless in Touliu"

Touliu

Week Eight

Paul dreamed that the tour was over, and the few remaining crewmembers were going home. They got to the airport, and in a waiting room, found all the people who had left early, looking very pale and gaunt. Their return tickets were invalid, but their visas had expired, so they had been kept in limbo for three months without food or water.

In reality, we faced our pull down without Robbie, our only experienced forklift driver. This meant a lot of back breaking work. One part was easy, though – the arch that our amazing welders built collapsed like a pop-up book.

The winds were high, and the crew had difficulty disconnecting the bail rings from the kingpoles. Paul climbed up with Mieczyslaw on one of the four sockets that the kingpoles fit through. Mieczyslaw had his own unique way of communicating: "You – up – whew-whew-whew – Ein, Zwei, pffft!" Which roughly translated as, "If a wind comes up, this thing will rip your legs off, so when I tell you to, jump!"

Mieczyslaw, Vaughan, Chris and a crew of Chinese workers travelled ahead to Kaohsiung with the tent, while the rest of us proceeded to Touliu, a small city in Yunlin County where the circus would perform for four days in an indoor sports arena. It was a joy to be working inside.

We arrived in mid-afternoon. The *Lonely Planet* guidebook described the Fortune Hotel as "luxury class". I would bear that in mind when considering their "basic" accommodations. When I pressed the doorbell of my room, it produced a sound resembling the mating call of the pterodactyl. Then Sweetpea answered. Yes, we were sharing, but only for one night. He had already checked out the amenities, including the usual array of TV cable channels – movies, CNN and soft-core porn.

Near the hotel were the essential staples of civilisation. Kentucky Fried Chicken. Pizza Hut. McDonald's. I asked the hotel concierge to direct me to the nearest bank. Indicating a leaflet that advertised "Citibank", I thought she understood. She leafed through a big book. I thought it might be a business directory of some sort but no, she was trying to find "Citibank" in a Chinese-English dictionary.

When I mailed my dispatches, I had a tough time making the post office clerk understand what an "Aerogramme" was. The fellow standing behind me was a

Christian missionary from Hong Kong and he offered to translate for me, but they didn't understand him either – he was Cantonese.

My hair was getting long and uncomfortable, but I was wary of having it cut by someone who might not understand what I wanted. (That, and the fear that it might not be a genuine barber shop.) It was time to take things in hand and wing it. Besides, it would be months before anybody who knew me would see me. I sat myself down, the lady barber draped a cloth over me, and her hands began to work my scalp in a way that made me understand why there was such a fine line between barber shops and, er, shall we say, other establishments. The hair cut was fine, but when it came to the beard, she didn't have the faintest idea. Few Chinese men had beards, so we left it alone.

When I arrived for my night shift, Mike and Al were setting the lights. While playing inside meant we didn't need to raise a tent or build up seating, it also meant a tougher job for those doing the rigging. They had to find a different place to mount the lighting, sound, trapeze, tight rope, nets, etc.

I scouted for a power lead so that I could hook up my word processor. "You won't need it," Mike snarled, "you'll be helping us." A 'please' would not have gone amiss.

About three in the morning, after Mike and Al left, the Chinese security guards shared their dinner

with me.   They offered whiskey and beer, but
although they spoke no English, I was able to make
them understand that I didn't drink alcohol.   They
kept giving me bags of "mooncakes", some stuffed
with apple which was nice, and something else with
an unknown vegetable – possibly tofu – that was
ghastly.

I found a quiet side room with wrestling mats.
It seemed to be the only restful place in all of Touliu.
So I took respite where I could get it.

When the crew arrived at eight, Vincent drove
me back to the hotel in his gold Mercedes-Benz. He
told me "You... different from others." I was not too
sure how to take that. It was certainly true that my
lifestyle was atypical, but I found that most of the
crew respected me for it. Being from such a mixed
bunch, including some strict Muslims, you might say
we were united in our diversity.

Our first night in Touliu on 12 December was a bit sparse. The stadium seated 8500 people. We were told that two shows were sold out in advance there, but evidently some bookings were cancelled. I don't think there were 8500 tickets sold for the entire six performances. Hsu claimed it cost him 100,000NT per day to keep the company of eighty in Taiwan, and our houses had never been good, further confirming that there was a cash flow problem. The original itinerary indicated a much longer stay here, but a booking in Chia-yi had been moved back and our stay in Kaohsiung brought forward. No explanation was offered.

I arrived for work just as the show was finishing. There was very little room back stage for turning the shifting boxes, and there was much merriment when one of the tigers peed through the bars in full view of the audience. Because our lighting was insufficient, the show had to be done with the house lights up. We weren't fooling anybody.

On the following day, Jill went to pick up our passports, with their extended visas, from the Yunlin Police Bureau, but they weren't there. Somebody from New Aspect had already claimed them. Although it is against international law to hold onto somebody's passport without just cause, she was afraid that Hsu would keep them as a bargaining chip, just as he allegedly had with Madame Maximova's. Somehow, she managed to get into their production office and steal them back.

On our last night in the arena, I saw evidence that Taiwan, while fast emerging as a first world economy, still had a third world mindset when it came to issues such as safety. To my horror, I learned that all of the fire exits had been locked throughout the run. Sadly, as the 1999 earthquake would later reveal, the country was long on regulation but short on compliance.

Such stories were by no means rare. I later spoke to a man who had been sent to one of Chaing Kai-shek's military training facilities while with the Malaysian army in the 1970s. When they were doing target practice, he was appalled to find people working in the rice fields in between the tanks and their targets.

I worked all night then caught the bus, another tight turnaround.

Act IV, Scene 2
"Chestnuts Roasting in an Open Sewer"

Week Nine

Kaohsiung

Now there was a heavenly sight. A circus tent, in the middle of a field, and I didn't have to lift a finger to raise it. I breathed the fresh air of liberty.

Or tried to. As I inhaled, I detected the unmistakable stench of methane gas. Behind the tent a river flowed so black and foamy that it looked like Coca-Cola on draft. This was just one of the many inspiring attributes of an area that, during World War II, had been the site of the Takao camp where prisoners of war were held awaiting shipment to Japan. It was a healthy reminder that, no matter how bad things were for us – there were others who'd had it a lot worse. What was once a dock land, heavily bombed by the allies, was now an industrial site, with a fertiliser factory and sugar storage facility nearby.

Yes, Kaohsiung was as polluted as it was prosperous. A million and a half people lived and worked in this, the third largest container port in the world, located just south of the Tropic of Cancer. Some of these people would, we hoped, be happy to see us. Some of them clearly were not.

A local businessman was angry to find a tent on "his" site. For years he had squatted – oops, I mean parked – his trucks there free of charge. He demanded many concessions, including a hefty percentage of our box office. He was paid off in time for our opening date of 18 December.

I wandered about in a fog. Although I had come straight off a night shift, sending me back to the hotel would have involved somebody making a decision. While a very charming and charismatic man – say, Nelson Mandela – could make one feel like you're the only person in the room, Mike had a way of making me feel I wasn't there at all. He had more important things on his mind. After an hour or so, he finally noticed me and let me go.

Lying in bed with my eyes wide open, daylight streaming in through the curtains, I counted no less than five cars with loudspeakers, all competing with each other. Many of them were advertising our show. Just how Mendelssohn's *Wedding March* related to this was unclear. On top of it all, somebody set off firecrackers.

Then the phone rang. A strange woman asked to speak to Vaughan. I told her she had the wrong room. After a few minutes, just as I was settling down to sleep, she called again. When I explained that Vaughan didn't live there, she "not understand". Vaughan explained later that she was his Taichung girlfriend. "Why is she calling me in Kaohsiung?" he mused. "Can't she see I've moved on?"

Unable to sleep, I turned on the television and surfed the choice of movies, Filipino game shows in pidgin English and who knew what. I finally settled on the Japanese national channel, NHK. This was the Sumo wrestling championships, a David and Goliath (Goliath and Goliath?) event if I ever saw one. Although there was no translation, none was necessary.

Their Hawaiian-born "Makuuchi", Konishiki was about to crash his six hundred fifty pound bulk – and his career – to the floor in defeat. Seeing a man the size of a Subaru move with agility, only to stumble and land with an earth-shaking thud on his outsized belly, was strangely therapeutic. I sent a picture to my mother with my head super-imposed onto Konishiki's body, with the caption: "Yes, Mom, I'm getting enough to eat."

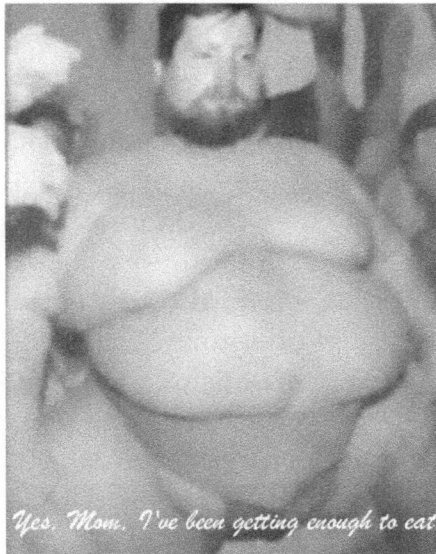

Yes, Mom, I've been getting enough to eat.

Then I tried again to catch up on sleep. Sweetpea burst into the room, took one look at my lethargic frame stretched out on the bed, and shouted "NO! I'm not havin' it!" and stormed out.

I wandered around the downtown harbour area, looking for a cinema. Suddenly, I was startled by the earache-inducing howl of a siren. Was this it? Had the mainland forces come to get us? But there were no fire engines and nobody scurrying about in a panic. I hadn't heard an air-raid test since the cold war days, but here, the cold war was still raging.

A young lad eagerly offered to help me in my quest for a cinema. Unfortunately, what I didn't realise was that I was only two blocks from the main cinema district, and he was leading me away from it.

I tried desperately to find a replacement printer ribbon for my ageing word processor. The internet revolution was just beginning, and although there were cyber-cafés everywhere, I didn't yet have an email address – and neither did most of the people I was writing to. Taiwan, where a third of the entire world's "motherboards" are produced, was far too high tech to understand such stone-age technologies as "daisy-wheel printers". The net result was that my letters home were becoming progressively fainter. Given the juxtaposition of a chaotic and uncertain future and my fading text, my friend James in Toronto wondered, "would Mel totally disappear?" I even put out an appeal for friends back home to send me a ribbon. One of them obliged, but sadly, it never reached me.

As I was getting ready to leave for work, there was a rapping at my door. It was Al. "I've got a small favour to ask." The crew had adopted a stray dog and named him Einstein. I agreed to keep an eye out for him.

This was a plague that had hit Taiwan in a big way. Parents would buy their children a puppy for Christmas – not for life. When they became bored with it, they simply abandoned the mongrel, and now the streets were crawling – literally – with cats and dogs. Wu-hung and his Life Conservationists were hot on the case, but it seemed that little progress had been made.

When I returned for my shift at one o'clock in the morning, I handed the taxi driver the flyer with the address of the site on it. He glanced at it with an illusion of comprehension, although he spoke no English. This fact almost allowed me to forgive him for the noise that emanated from his stereo.

On his tape deck was playing a "song" that I later learned was called "I Want to F*** You Like An Animal," although if it had been up to me, I would have given it a less genteel title. By a band called "Nine Inch Nails", it consisted of an incessant electronic drum beat, and a woman's voice screaming "I really want to f*** you" over and over again, with the odd variation – "F*** your brains out!" I began to visualise the creative process that had gone into this magnum opus. The lyricist is struggling to find just the right word. He accidentally stabs himself with his pen. Writhing in pain, he lets slip the requisite expletive, then exclaims "Eureka! That's it! That's the word I was looking for!" As one who has spent his life polishing his lyrical craft, studying the fine art of the perfect rhyme and of a sophisticated turn of phrase, I was struck dumb. No critical analysis was possible. I thought, surely there was a universally accepted standard that says that this was crap.[22] What cocaine ravaged A&R man had listened to that and said, "This is vibrant and exciting stuff"? Clearly the likes of Ira Gershwin would never have been able to make it in today's cutthroat, competitive music industry. This was clearly the product of a lower life form, one whose acid soaked brain had been pulped by a cricket bat. What sort of sparkling rhyme would Johnny Mercer have contributed? "You're out of luck, you"? "Tar, feather and pluck you"? I wanted to throw my copy of *Sammy Cahn's Rhyming Dictionary* out the window.

If I had done so, it would have landed in the middle of nowhere, because that's where I was. The flyer gave only the nearest major intersection. As I said, empty fields don't have house numbers.

At this point, the language barrier began to be a problem (to put it mildly). Every time I said, "No, this isn't it" and tried to point the way, the driver stepped on the accelerator and got me further lost.

---

[22] I was wrong. One of my musical colleagues offered the following defence: "It expresses musically and lyrically what it's like to be a degraded sex pervert or a serial killer. That is something Musical Theatre could never do." Let's be grateful for small mercies.

Perhaps he couldn't understand the word "stop", but I thought that the traditional hand signal – miming slitting his throat – was pretty universal. Evidently it was not, and I simply screamed until the glass in his windows began to shake loose. I'd had more meaningful conversations with my cat. When he stopped the car, I got out and left him without paying.

After an hour or so of wandering about and crying "I want my Mum", I found a young woman who said, in broken English, "I take you there." I hopped on the back of her friend's motor scooter while she led the way, and was at the site in five minutes. (Once I got away from the circus, I found the Taiwanese people would give you the shirts off their backs.)

I looked around for Einstein, but there was no sign of him. "Ooh, there'll be tears at bed time over this", Jill said later.

Although we were in a tropical climate, it could still get cool at night. I sat in the workshop container freezing, with my sweatshirt, sweater and jacket on, pulling my sleeves up to keep my hands warm. The one saving grace was that there were no mosquitoes. I spent the whole night with my hands shivering, forgetting that I had my work gloves in my pocket. It's not a nice feeling to realise you are not the brightest bulb on the tree.

One of my new jobs was to feed the horses in the morning. These animals were no longer part of the circus but were merely being kept on site until Hsu found a buyer. Horribly neglected, they had no qualified grooms, got very little exercise, were often left tied to the fence out in the sun, and their stalls were so poorly built they had cuts in their flanks from rubbing the exposed nails. I took pictures of them to keep as an insurance policy.

In the morning, my relief arrived two hours late, choosing to wait for the bus rather than take a cab. I was off to the hotel to have some token sleep, careful not to appear too energetic.

In the absence of Arny, I tried to re-impose our roster, but nobody else was interested. "Must you be so pedantic?" moaned Paul. I was stung. As a result, some of my colleagues chose to turn up for work as and when they felt like it. I was doing steady night shifts. Originally, this was so that Chris could finish rebuilding some seating for Paul on the day shift. However, I found that the night shift was the only time that I got any peace and quiet.

Back at the hotel, René, leader of the Mexican trapeze flyers, stayed in the room across the hall, and had just bought himself a new CD/DVD stereo system. I couldn't make the hotel staff understand that I worked shifts. The cleaners came in to my room to do the beds. When they turned the lights on, I shrieked at them, but they pointed at me and laughed. (Only later did I learn that a Chinese laugh could mean embarrassment rather than ridicule.)

My father offered me his sympathy. In his first job away from home, he was stuck in a boarding house next to a guy who played cowboy music all day long.

As I bounded out of the hotel to go exploring, Jill eyed me suspiciously. "Aren't you tired?" she said. "Sure I am," I lied. "But what's the point in trying to sleep in there?"

In spite of its pollution, Kaohsiung did have a few redeeming qualities. In fact, it had areas that bordered on being scenic. A short walk of about 1km brought me to Wanshoushan ("Mount Longevity") Park, opened to the public in 1988. A trail led up to a lookout at 328 metres, giving me a view of the city. I stopped, intending to buy film but, at 750 NT, the price was so extortionate, I decided to pass. Atop the mountain was the Martyrs' Shrine, built to commemorate the Chinese who died fighting for their country.

On my way, I passed John Everett, another member of our crew, who'd come up to sketch the view.

Continuing on, I came to a long foot tunnel beneath the mountain, which led to the campus of National Sun Yat-sen University. This was formerly the site of Chiang Kai-Shek's retreat. Nearby was a small fishing harbour with a cement sea wall, and Hsitzuwan Beach. On a hilltop overlooking the bay was the former British Consulate. Built in 1858, it was Taiwan's first foreign diplomatic mission, but was abandoned when Japan took possession of the island. Afterward it became a weather station, and was now a museum. From there I took a passenger ferry across the harbour to Chichen Island, home of Tienhou Temple, built in 1691. Unfortunately, by the time I got there, it was dark. I bought dinner from a street stall, and headed back to work.

I had heard that the Lotus Pond at Tsoying was an interesting spot, so the next day I decided to walk the seven kilometres to get there.

En route, I witnessed a nasty accident in which a motor cyclist was knocked down onto the pavement. He lay still, his face covered in blood. I went to see if there was anything I could do. A small crowd gathered around. As he regained consciousness, I said, "Stay still". For all he understood, I might as well have said, "Let's dance". He got up, got back on his bike and rode off.

As I approached the Lotus Pond – actually the city reservoir – I found it to be surrounded by a park, with temples and pagodas reaching out into the lake. At the north end was Taiwan's largest Confucius temple, built in a pastiche of Sung dynasty style. Here, each 28 September the annual Teachers Day was celebrated, marking the great master's birthday. I passed the Spring and Autumn pavilions built in 1951 to commemorate Kuan Kung, the god of war. Given that it was built at the beginning of Chiang Kai-Shek's exile on Taiwan, the symbolism was not subtle, and the presence of a statue of Kuanyin, the goddess of mercy out front was certainly ironic.   Further down, I stopped at the Dragon and Tiger Pagodas. I walked in through the dragon's mouth, the interior of which was decorated with scenes of heaven and hell, meant to inspire good behaviour. I emerged from the tiger's mouth – meant to turn bad luck into good.

Then I made my way to Tsoying station, and caught a train back into the city centre.

Using the shifting boxes to move the tigers from their cages into the ring was a cumbersome operation, so Phillip faxed very precise plans to Vincent for a tiger tunnel, an interlocking series of cages that would form a secure passageway. It sounded simple. Vincent glanced over the plans, relating what he could remember of them to our welders *par excellence*, who then constructed it with their usual flourish. The dimensions were all wrong, so I was asked to help Martin the Gnome to rebuild it.

Natasha the "dog lady"[23] watched, her arms folded in front of her. She muttered something in

---

[23] With her, "dog lady" wasn't a disparaging term –it was her job. She trained the Chihuahuas.

Russian. He laughed it off, until he realised she was trying to make a very good suggestion. Rather than cutting the bars off at the now lower height, why not bend them over and weld them together so that they formed the roof? As he did this, she beamed triumphantly.

Then she grabbed us. "You, coffee!" This was not so much an invitation as an order. She sat us down in her trailer and fed us toast and eggs until we were ready to burst, not letting us go until we'd eaten a full load.

For the moment, Greg and Gedda were still in Taiwan. Gedda had lost his ticket. KLM would replace it, but only for the original return date of 25 April, and his visa would expire before then. They'd had some under the counter work taking down Christmas decorations. The New Aspect management didn't know about any of this.

Although our contracts stipulated that we should be paid each Thursday, New Aspect changed the day to Friday, making it more difficult for me to send my money home. Even at that, Fiona, Mr. Hsu's assistant "didn't make it to the bank" as the dog had clearly eaten all of her deposit slips, so we had to wait.

Consequently, the company refused to do a promotion in the morning. In fact, nobody would do any work until they were paid. Except me: I didn't work because the cab driver got lost – we were in the wrong end of the city. I thought, "I don't remember going through mountains before..." At least he was honest, and didn't charge me.

On Saturday, we received our money at last, and Gavin grabbed his radio mic, snarling once again: **"Ladies and Gentlemen, Boys and Girls, welcome to the A-MER-i-can Un-i-VER-sal CIR-cus!"**

Act IV, Scene 3
If This Were Any More Ironic, it Would Rust

Week Ten

Being a non-Christian country, December 25 was technically known as Constitution Day, but the shops couldn't get too excited about that idea. Instead, they were festooned in holiday glitter. Everywhere I went, I heard nauseating disco interpretations of Christmas songs. The voices dreamed of a white Christmas while I walked around in a sweatshirt. "You are dreaming", I thought with only mosquitoes, not Jack Frost, nipping at my nose. I hadn't laughed so much at a song since the marching band in front of a scandal-ridden Buckingham Palace played "The Lady is a Tramp".

All this synthetic Christmas cheer was making me ho-ho-homicidal. I needed a break, and this time it called for desperate measures. Because the rota had been abandoned, I didn't get a day off. Two days after Christmas, as soon as I came off the night shift, I hailed a cab to the airport. The guy who stopped was off duty and taking his wife there, so he gave me a lift gratis. (Once we got away from the New Aspect hierarchy, the Taiwanese people were incredibly generous.)

The flight to Makung via Great China Airlines in a DeHavilland Dash 8, took only thirty minutes, and cost 1500 NT (about £30) for a day trip. Although it was possible to get there by ferry, in the winter it was not advisable, due to high winds.

Penghu, sometimes known by its Portuguese name the "Pescadores", is an archipelago of 64 islands in the Taiwan Straits about half way to the mainland, a sort of Chinese Isle of Wight. Although the Chinese had claimed them even before they claimed Taiwan, they had also been occupied by more foreign imperialists. The chain had been seized by Japanese pirates in the sixteenth century, and was the base for the Dutch invasion of Taiwan. Even the French had their moment in its wind-swept sun.

The tiny airport at Makung looked more like a bus station. Outside, I found a dark-skinned woman in sunglasses beckoning me toward her cab. A ten-minute ride brought me to the centre of Makung.

What I really came to see was Tienhou, the "temple of the Queen of Heaven", the oldest Matsu temple in Taiwan. Built in the early days of the Ming dynasty – fifteenth century – it was originally known as Niang-ma Kung, "temple of the honourable mother". Following a sixteenth century Japanese occupation, it was rebuilt and renamed T'ien-pei, "Princess of Heaven". It was enlarged again when Yu

Ta-yu defeated the Japanese in 1563, and again in 1592 when the Ming armies repelled the Japanese yet again. Then in 1622 the Dutch arrived, building a fort on Penghu to mount their commercial and military assault on Taiwan. Two years later, Yu Tzu-kao drove them out and remodelled the temple again. When in 1683 Shin Lang captured Penghu for the Ch'ing dynasty, he expressed his gratitude to Matsu, goddess of the sea, by elevating her status from Princess to Queen. Renovations continued throughout the eighteenth and nineteenth centuries until its complete restoration in 1923.

The temple was small and austere by Taiwanese standards. Built on a slope, a flight of stone steps led up to the entrance, shaded by a large tree. Inside I met a young Taiwanese couple who now lived in San Francisco. It was refreshing to be able to talk to somebody who spoke English fluently – just to be able to have a two-way conversation. I stayed a few minutes inside the temple looking up at its high, wide curved roof, inlaid with encaustic tiles.

I walked around the town, through its ancient gate and out toward Lintou Beach. The fields, which grew peanuts, sweet potatoes and sorghum, were hemmed in by dry stone walls, protecting them from the high winds that constantly battered the islands in winter. I was lucky, for on this day, it was unseasonably calm. Penghu had few trees, only shrubs. The beauty was only slightly spoiled by a heavy military presence, being only a few miles from the Chinese mainland.

At Lintou Beach, I had a chance to dip my feet in the Pacific Ocean from its western side for the first time. On the beach, which was formed of pumice-like gravel, almost like coral, I found the remains of a defensive pillbox. It looked old and weathered enough to have been Japanese. While I didn't bring a bathing suit, I waded in up to my knees.

Nearby I found a cage with a monkey in it. A zoo, I thought. Another cage had a chicken. The one next to it had – another chicken. There were twenty more cages – all filled with chickens, with a monkey standing guard.

There was a very impressive military cemetery next to the beach. Around this were some very elaborate floral gardens – a pleasant break from the rocky shoreline.

A moment of peace, and a chance to think. Several friends suggested I might find inspiration in Taiwan for a musical. Although I didn't feel the world needed another *Jumbo*, stranger things had happened (and would yet). At this point in my life, inspiration was something I was in desperate need of. After scribbling a "middle C" onto a fresh stave, and confidently inserting the word "the" beneath it, I was lost.

Perhaps herein lay the answer. When the muse deserts you, there's nothing quite like going "oingo-boingo" at the ends of the earth. Or, as my friend Norman Campbell put it, "Withal, through all life's adventures, remember how great you'll be as a talk show guest!!!"

While it was interesting, I couldn't say the day was all that relaxing. By this time, I had come to understand that the Chinese did not place the same premium on peace, quiet and serenity as Westerners did. I figured the Buddha must have known how to enjoy life – you don't get to be that size on rice and water alone.

I lay on the beach for an hour before walking to the airport and flying back to work. So much for my jet set lifestyle. It was back to reality, such as it was.

Act IV, Scene 4

"How Much for Prostitution?"

Week Eleven

The Chinese called 1998 the "Year of the Tiger". I looked forward to never finding out why.

On New Years' Day[24], I was probably the only sober person with white skin in all of Kaohsiung. With all the partying going on, I got very little sleep. Not that I was partying.

Although I did not participate in the festivities, rumour of their excesses – like some grade Z rock and roll band on tour in the hinterlands and bored – filtered down to me. Yuri wandered the halls in a robotic stupor, asking the hotel staff, "How much for prostitution?" Sweetpea showed off his British reserve by dropping his drawers in the nearby 7Eleven. The Chinese staff asked Yi, "Why are they being so obnoxious?" Why, indeed.

I was awakened at an early hour by Boris' thundering voice, arguing with a yet more inebriated Yuri.

---

[24] Although they used the Western calendar (for day and month, but not for year), 1 January was no big deal to the Taiwanese. Their New Year celebration came about four weeks later.

"ЮРИ, НЕТ!"

As I left for work, Sweetpea was sitting on the steps of the hotel, bellowing his greetings to the bemused passers-by. I snarled at him as I passed.

I pulled into the circus site. Jill came up to me, put her arms around me and hugged me. "Happy New Year!" she chirped. By this time, I had become firmly ensconced as the resident über-grouch. I was not feeling so chirpy, and I'm sure that my body language – stiff as a mannequin and cuddly as a cactus – communicated that fact quite effectively. In spite of more than two decades in the theatre, I'd never been comfortable with being hugged by people I was not on intimate terms with. So I cut to the chase.

With an air of dismay, she cried, "You can't tell him not to have a social life!" At the risk of sending my popularity rating to subterranean levels, I pointed out, "Yes I can, actually. There is a sobriety clause in all our contracts." She rolled her eyes. The touchy-feely luviedom of her recent *auld lang syne* quickly evaporated. As if it were some unwritten tenet of class-consciousness, she implied that Sweetpea's right to carouse took precedence over my right to sleep. I in turn implied that I might have to reconsider my position.

"I understand", she said. Oops. That was not how it was supposed to go.

Jill and Mike had a knack for letting me know just how unimportant I was. The only time I received my post was when somebody from Phillip's office in Cheshire came over, which was less than once a month. (I wasn't the only person with this problem. Martin, an asthmatic, was waiting for his inhalers, which were in the post from England.) Although I had important things like bank statements to worry about, I was not worth the price of a stamp to them. I was also owed over 5,000 NT[25] in cab fares, but whenever I came to them with a problem, I was treated as an irritant.

I was told that if I wanted to have my own room, I would have to pay 1400 NT[26] a week for it. Even at that, I could only do it if Sweetpea agreed to pay the same supplement. Otherwise, no deal. I walked away in silence. I was left with little recourse. I would now deal with the problem in whatever way worked for me.

Come show time, Yuri was still sailing, and love was in the air. Greg and Kat were looking for a priest to marry them, while Jill was sporting Mike's ring.

That night, the Large Mammal once again merrily sawed logs. "Sweetpea!" I shouted, "stop snoring!" "Okay". And he did. Apparently, all I had to do was ask.

---

[25] £100
[26] £28

In the morning, a more subdued Yuri was heard muttering "Vodka, nyet. Milk, da." Where were the firecrackers and loudspeakers when I needed them?

Two days later, Greg (still unmarried) and Gedda left for old Blighty. Greg's back had not recovered, and he had also twisted his ankle, but without Gedda, we were now reduced to one electrician. This almost became irrelevant, because the hire firm came to take back the generators that Hsu hadn't paid the rent on. A few hours later, a different firm brought a new set.

Al, our chief electrician, and Tigger, his girlfriend decided they'd also had enough. He knew he had offers back home. "If this were a good tour I'd stay," he said, "but it's not. Will you miss me?" "Probably", I answered, "but, then again, I never was a very good aim."

A theatrical superstition says that a good dress rehearsal can mean a woeful first night. Does the same thing apply to pull-downs? We had our smoothest one yet in Kaohsiung, but rumours abounded that New Aspect had run out of money, and that we wouldn't be paid unless we handed over our tickets and passports.

Act V, Scene 1
"S'truth, This Place is Fulla White People!"

Chia-yi

Week Twelve

Jill gave me a big build up about how nice our hotel room was going to be in Chia-Yi. This was her way of preparing me for the fact that I was still going to be sleeping next to the Sweetpeaosauras Rex. I told her I was glad of this. I wanted us to stay together indefinitely, so that I could complete my psychological experiments.

According to our original itinerary, we should have been in Tainan, a much bigger town, but it seemed it was cancelled or postponed. The cowards.

Judging by the abandoned buildings, it seemed the site here had been a military camp of some kind. I suggested that it might have been American. "Then why do they have a statue of Chiang Kai-shek?" asked Chris. "Look more closely. That's not Chiang Kai-shek," I suggested, "that's Walt Disney."

The military trappings aside, Chia-Yi looked promising. It was the main transit point for Taiwan's mountain resorts. Of course, two years later, when it was the epicentre of the disastrous 1999 earthquake, I was glad to be safe in my Bloomsbury flat, but at this point in our trip, I was ready for some real scenery.

Raising and lowering the kingpoles was the most dangerous part of the operation. Paul rolled his eyes wearily as he watched the king poles go up. Mieczyslaw decided that they could be raised entirely by cranes, without anyone pumping the tirfors[27]. "Slow and steady," muttered Paul, "slow and steady...", shaking his head in disapproval as they careered about. "I don't like to criticise another tent master, but..."

The good news was that Vincent had arrived with lunch. The bad news was that we were expected to eat it. With the lukewarm takeaway pork-on-the-bone with rice and cabbage, this was not possible. Some strange and nauseous liquid came with it in a sealed plastic bag that looked like a water balloon. Was it intended to be hot, or had it just been left out in the sun? To drink it, we were meant to stab a straw through the skin and suck. The vegetarians among us were given the same meal without the pork.

Enough of this. We demanded McDonald's. Except the Moroccans, who were all observing Ramadan, the ninth month of the Islamic calendar. This meant that they fasted from sunrise to sunset. And still they worked faster than we did.

---

[27] Tirfors, or griphoists, are a type of winche that uses self-gripping jaws. By moving a handle back and forth, one person can lift objects several tons in weight.

At least the horses were getting exercised again. All work stopped when the beauteous Christina was seen riding them around the site, her luxurious chestnut hair bobbing in the breeze. She still wasn't being paid, but she missed riding so much she could stand it no longer.

I was even given a chance to drive a forklift. And although I didn't knock any buildings over, the look on Paul's face said, "Come back, Robbie, all is forgiven".

It was a twenty-minute walk back to the hotel. There was no bus. (Another unpaid bill?) En route, I went in to the corner store to buy my fix of Coca-Cola and ice cream. At the same time, a group of railway engineers from Perth entered and spotted me and proclaimed loudly, "S'truth – this place is fulla white people!" Not me. I was a deep shade of crimson.

My suitcase was full of muddy jeans, tee shirts, socks and underwear that I had been living in for the past three days. I left them with the concierge to be sent out with the hotel laundry.

Then, I shocked everybody by shaving my beard off. Paul greeted me with "F***in' hell! Just because the hotel gives you free razor blades..." Not true. I'd always wanted to know what I would look like shaving with a sunburned face. I called it my five o'clock sunbeam. And it was a chance to do it while clogging up somebody else's plumbing.

When calling home, the time difference between Taiwan and Vancouver was sixteen hours. It was hard to remember whether that was ahead or behind. On this occasion, I got it spectacularly wrong. My father answered with a "...huh...?" A few days later, I received a letter from him. "Even if it was 5 AM and neither Marion or I had been able to go to sleep before 2, (are you feeling guilty enough yet?) it was good to hear your voice."

When I picked up my laundry the following morning, I was presented with a bill for 1000 NT[28]. They had dry-cleaned my underwear, blue jeans and socks.

---

[28] About £20.

Act V, Scene 2

I've Grown Accustomed to this Farce

Week Thirteen

Friday. Pay day. Sigh. The rumours were true. There would be no pay unless we handed over our travel documents. Too many deserters, Ken said. If ever there was a signal to "git while the gittin's good", this was it.

As was the custom, we each entered the room one at a time, while our colleagues waited outside. Gavin, much the worse for booze, swaggered in screaming obscenities, to apparently great effect. He stumbled out, cried "Oops! I forgot my money!" and went back in.

When Paul's turn came up, we strained to hear what was being said. His voice boomed **"Sit down or I'll put you down!"** Then he tried to make a grab for his money, but after about three-quarters of an hour, he stormed out empty handed.

By then, the artists had all been paid, but not the crew. Mr. Hsu had decided to single us out for exclusion. I was tempted to hand in the leftover ticket voucher from my flight to Penghu, just to see if they'd notice the difference.

Ultimately, those of us who remained went in together and confronted Ken and Fiona. Everybody spoke at once, alcohol being a cardinal influence. Fiona cried "Please! English not my native language!" I wanted to scream "Shut up, everyone!" as discipline collapsed.

The following morning, I put in a call to the Canadian Trade Office in Taipei, where I left a message with the head of consular affairs, advising him of my situation. They asked if I needed a place to stay, but for now I was all right.

Alice told me that Greg and Gedda were now safely home. They were able to persuade KLM to change their flight even without the original tickets. "Hmm," I said, "That's a useful piece of information." Her face lit up as the implications of this dawned on her. "Oh yeah! Right!"

As it stood, nobody was doing any more work, except for me. Some people thought I'd broken rank, but I'd merely agreed to protect the animals. However, I did have one great moment of satisfaction.

When I arrived on site, I found that the small petrol generator had somehow walked away. The only way I would have light to work by was if I fired up the main diesel power plant. Since I didn't know the wiring arrangements, it was absolutely necessary for me to leave all the show lights, festoons and spotlights on. There were fireworks as I dragged the dodgy extension leads along the wet ground.

Fiona, Ken and Professor Lu came to see me at the site, hoping to persuade me to toe the line. I considered the possibility of handing in my ticket, safe in the knowledge that KLM would honour the reservation anyway. But it hardly mattered. They found me sitting in the middle of a field, reading a book under a fifteen-hundred-watt halogen lamp. I would like to think that the value of the fuel I burned that night was at least equal to the amount of money they owed me.

Would we be paid? Would the show open on Saturday? Who knew? In the meanwhile, I planned to reformat Sweetpea's brain.

Act V, Scene 2
"NO BUSINESS LIKE HSU BUSINESS"

The Following Day

I expected to be surprised. I did not expect to be gob-smacked. But, it finally happened: Hsu sacked the entire British crew and ordered us to be out of our hotel by noon. He claimed to have a court order banning Mike and Paul from coming within 100 metres of the tent.

"But what about our contracts?" I asked. I'd been engaged for a six-month tour. "It's not worth the paper it's written on" replied somebody whom I'd sure had never been within a hundred yards of a law school. "Oh, I'll sue", I swore. "You'd better believe it. They've never seen such sue-age as they're gonna get from me!"

Phillip handed Hsu an ultimatum that if he did not pay $US25,000 by Wednesday, the tent was coming down. Hsu had also not remitted any commission on the artist's fees. The show went on without us, with the Moroccans and the Russians doing the props.

Although we were not being paid, Phillip took care of our hotel bills and asked us to stay in case we were needed to pull the tent.

Some of our crew found their way up to the roof of the hotel and began partying. Afraid of offending the manager, Mike and Jill warned them not to get too drunk. They needn't have worried: the manager soon came up with a case of beer, a bag of ice, and some snacks. His generosity did not end there: he gave us vouchers for a free all-you-can-eat breakfast for each morning we were there.

People began to talk about the trip home, as if it were a fait accomplis. It would be a few days before we could get a flight out, if we left. There was also a suggestion of extending our stopover in Bangkok on the return journey. We'd heard you could live cheap, eat well, and some of the guys wanted to confirm the stories they'd heard of the amazing and exotic feats Thai women could do with Ping-Pong balls...

In due time, Vincent offered to give us our jobs back if we promised in writing that we would stay with the show. Some of us seriously considered this. Mike and Jill contended, "If you still think things are going to get better, you're naive." I asked Mike to fax the proposal to Phillip's lawyer. He retorted, "So you think I'm full of shit?" He seemed to want to find something offensive in whatever I said. I calmly spelled out that, no, I respected and valued his opinion, but I wanted to try to salvage my job, even if it was a lost cause. Nobody could accuse us of rearranging the deck chairs on the "Titanic". Not when our tickets clearly said "Andrea Doria".

Mike acquiesced and sent the fax. Referring to us as the "young Mafia", Hsu later added another condition: that we work strictly for him, by-passing Phillip. This would have been illegal.

There are worse places in the world to be stuck than in Chia-Yi, in the centre of Taiwan's mountain resort district. Alishan, Tungpu and Sun-Moon Lake were all nearby. Here Paul joined me as I indulged my fascination with railways once again. The Alishan Forest Railway, begun by the Japanese in 1901 to haul logs and opened in 1912, was one of the great railway engineering feats. As the line was narrow gauge – two and a half foot – it had its own separate station in Chia-Yi. In fact, there were two – the current building was a plain concrete structure that probably dated from the 1960s, while the original Japanese wooden building lay derelict. An earlier generation of rolling stock was parked rusting away on a siding while passengers rode modern (1980s) cars with upholstered reclining seats.

The tropic of cancer runs through this region, and so the climate of Chia-yi, at an altitude of 30 metres above sea level, is semi-tropical. This was reflected in the palm trees that I saw through the train's windows as we passed through sugar fields. As we climbed, these gave way to conifers, and the temperature plummeted. Fenchihu, at 1400 metres, was roughly two-thirds of the way to Alishan, but it was the furthest I could go and still return the same day.

One Taiwanese website describes the journey in verbiage that could only be concocted by somebody with English as a thirty-second language: "Circling mountain and warming itself into tunnels, striding valley with birds hovering below the train wheels..."[29] Hoping that no feathers would get tangled around the axles delaying the journey, I pressed on. Although I would miss some of the fifty tunnels and eighty bridges on the line, it was still an invigorating ride. In some cases, I could look down precipices on both sides of the train as it rode over a crest, surrounded by the Dawu range of eighteen major mountains straddling Nantou and Chia-yi counties.

As we pulled into the small station at Fenchihu ("Get-up Lake"), I found an engine house at the end of the platform. Inside, I could just make out three small steam locomotives – all Shays built in 1914 in Lima, Ohio. This was the sort of thing that makes a rail enthusiast's heart go pitta-pat.

---

[29] www.toptrip.cc/destination/spot/tw_alishan.html

Paul tried hard to relax and enjoy himself, but I could see by his eyes that he just couldn't. I took a deep breath of fresh mountain air and thought, "It's so quiet, and not a loudspeaker in ear shot." Just then, a van with loudspeakers on its roof rounded a corner joyously announcing itself. Serenity was an alien concept: even here there were the ubiquitous KTV clubs.

We made the return trip to Chia-Yi on a somewhat less inspiring rickety old bus with no suspension. When I got home, I called my railfan father in Canada to tell him I'd just ridden on one of the great railway journeys of the world. "Go drop on your big fat head", he said.

That evening, Mr. Hsu and Ken came into the hotel foyer and saw me sitting with Paul. Hsu asked me to come and speak to him. Paul pointed and said, "There's a seat right here", but Hsu clearly didn't want to talk in front of him. I said "Anything you want to say to me you can say in front of Paul." They left.

Ken spotted me at breakfast on Tuesday. He ushered me over to his table, then told me that if I came up to his hotel room, he would pay me. There were no conditions, except that I was not to tell anybody. He claimed that Phillip had received his money. (In fact, Phillip had received only five thousand dollars.)

I went to his room, where he was good for his word. I immediately sent the money to my account in London. Then I went straight to Paul and said, "I'm not supposed to tell you that I've been paid, so I won't."

Asserting that I still had a job, I reported to work that night. I was determined to fulfil the letter of my contract, ensuring that New Aspect would have no just grounds to stop paying me. Yuri and Victor were there, and followed me wherever I went. "All for one, one for all" my arse.

Finally, Professor Lu turned up and asked me to leave on Ken's orders. Both sides suspected each other would sabotage the tent.

Phillip called a meeting of the crew. Deciding to let lying dogs sleep, he would not pull the tent. There would be no point. Taiwanese law forbade him to ship it back to England, even although New Aspect had not paid up. He would have been required to store it within the court's jurisdiction for the duration of the contract, and to post a bond equal to New Aspect's estimate of its lost earnings. This bond might far exceed the tent's value.

It seemed that, just like the time he accused Mike and Jill of stealing our wages, the plane ticket issue was another bizarre smoke screen. The solicitor Phillip engaged in Taipei was the same one who sued New Aspect on behalf of the *Great European Circus* two years earlier. While he won in court, he collected nothing because all of New Aspect's assets were vested in another company called New Aspect Promotions Corporation. Phillip thought that he might as well try to keep as many people in work as possible, although Hsu wanted to make drastic staff cuts, keeping only a handful of us. My name was mentioned. As a compromise, we could lodge our tickets with our respective pseudo-embassies. I had already made the Canadian Trade Office in Taipei aware of my situation.

In the end, only about half of our crew were paid. Hsu had successfully divided and conquered, Boris refusing even to speak to Phillip. Paul wasn't bitter. He said the Russians were merely doing what they had to do to survive, whereas I was tempted to remind them that we still had missiles pointed at them. But Boris was made of pragmatic Russian stoicism. He had a home in Moscow, but he also had one in Brussels.

With all their spare time, our people continued pairing and re-pairing. Now that Gedda was gone, Alice was with Tom – while those of us with all the sex appeal of a broken paving stone were out riding trains and sightseeing. The less sensible rented motor scooters, unscrupulously trying to lure me into their caper. I protested, "I don't have a licence". "You don't need one", Sweetpea countered. "I don't know how to ride a motor-bike," I said. Again, I was told it didn't matter. That was the part that frightened me. It meant that none of the other idiots on the road knew what they were doing either.

But however desolate things were, this was a part of the world I would not be likely to see again, so I made the most of it. The Chichi Railway line was an anachronism in the high tech world of modern Taiwan; a reminder of a simpler but less prosperous time. Its 1950s diesel rail cars were certainly a far cry from the immaculate new trains that plied between Kaohsiung and Taipei. With the creature comforts of a school bus, these weren't even third class, but they had charm oozing from their smelly exhaust and axle grease. The informality was further punctuated by the railway's habit of running with the doors open. But this was no high-speed train. This was more redolent of the Titfield Thunderbolt.

The train wheezed and gasped to a halt at Shuili station, where I alighted. This market town, whose name meant "in the water", was so called because market gatherings would take place in the river valley. Like nearby Alishan, this was a logging area, and was once so prosperous it was known as "Little Shanghai". It was also noted for its Ch'ing Dynasty pottery. Now it was a transfer point for tourists bound for Alishan, Sun-Moon Lake and Tung-pu, where I was headed by bus.

Tung-pu, at an altitude of 1120 metres, was a small collection of garish high rise hotels built on the side of a mountain near a hot spring. It was also the home of the Bunun aboriginal community. In the 1970s, the KMT government developed it as a tourist resort, but when the hotels were built, poverty forced the Bunun to sell their water rights. Since then, they'd been fighting for greater access to the hot springs.

From Tung-pu, I climbed up a long footpath to the spectacular "Caihóng Pùbù", or Rainbow Waterfall. The scene was only slightly spoiled by the mess of wires and pipes strewn across the path, but I learned that these were meant to carry water from the Rainbow Springs down to the Bunun reserve. Towering over Tung-pu is Yushan, at 3,952 metres, Taiwan's tallest mountain.

When I arrived back that evening, Sweetpea, back from his motor-scooter expedition, limped toward me, his arm in a sling and his body covered in bandages. "You should have come with us. It was fun."

And then, a four-hundred-sixty-pound soprano loosened up her tonsils and performed an aria – (metaphorically speaking).

Finale:

"Just Because You're Paranoid Doesn't Mean There Isn't Somebody After You"

Week Fourteen

"It can't get no worse than this" moaned Sweetpea, waking me. Vincent, Ken and another Chinese gentleman allegedly came into Chris' room about three o'clock in the morning and began punching him. They complained that he'd been to their booking office demanding his money, and generally stirring up a rumpus. They were also not happy that he was dating Camille, a member of Hsu's staff. They apparently warned him that if he did not leave Taiwan, they would make him "disappear". Hsu and Ken later denied all knowledge of this, even although the threat was repeated in front of Mike and Phillip. The police were called, but Vincent claimed that it was Chris who had attacked him. No action was taken.

Mike resigned. Jill booked a flight for all of the British crew, save Sweetpea and Martin, to fly back to London on Monday. All through the show, we had stuck it out, believing that things would get better. Now we had to concede that they were getting worse.

Sweetpea claimed he was only staying to protect Phillip's tent.

So far, I had stayed because I wanted to see how the story would end. Well, if this wasn't the ending, I didn't want to know what was. Paul, Mike and Jill wanted to move out of the hotel straight away because they didn't feel safe there. As Paul said, "Just because you're paranoid doesn't mean there isn't somebody after you." I warned before that the climb down over the plane tickets and money was enormous, and that the humiliation they would feel could become dangerous. I was right.

We would have to forego Hsinchu, Ping-tung, Tainan, Hualien, Taoyuan and Miao-li. I would miss exploring the more scenic East Coast.

Bill and Bob, the American clowns, tried to escape, but Professor Lu saw them heading off with their trunks and stopped them. They swore they'd try again, and several other acts were expected to follow. New Aspect realised that their layoffs left them without a forklift driver, so they tried to recruit Vaughan (at three o'clock in the morning!) On Phillip's advice, Vaughan pretended to go along with them, but he just wanted to collect his money and go.

The night before we left Chia-yi, there was a party in Marie's hotel room. Hsu invited Vaughan out to dinner with the New Aspect staff, saying he would pay him after the rest of us left. When Vincent came looking for him, Vaughan hid in Marie's closet.

Somebody had let the air out of the tires of Vincent's Mercedes. Nobody was saying anything, but everyone had his or her suspicions.

At breakfast, we said our good-byes to those who were staying behind. I decided to catch an earlier train to Taipei in one last attempt to see the National Palace Museum.

The bilingual sign in the railway station pointed to the "Excess Farz Office – Certificte of Purchasing Ticket". "I know English" the gentleman next to me on the train beamed. "I listen to BBC World Service". My skin colour was still a magnet for the curious. Lucky for him I wasn't Estonian. Or Basque. I told him there were still many things I'd like to see, including a Chinese Opera, and the National Palace Museum. He gave me a card with a phone number on it – written in Chinese, of course.

What I didn't realise was that the passenger trains on the West Coast main line terminated at Keelung, not Taipei. I was so loaded with luggage that the train pulled out before I was able to get off. When I arrived at the next station, Sungshan, some other passengers helped me cross over the tracks on a footbridge with my bags to catch the train heading back to Taipei.

When I reached my destination, a young seminary student named Wu Huey-Shin helped me into the station. I was unable to get cash out of the bank machine, so she bought me a bowl of soup, and remained with me for quite a long time. I think she must have been majoring in the parable of the Good Samaritan.

Paul had suggested, "Just meet under the clock. That always works", but the station had more clocks than a Seiko warehouse. I looked for a locker to store my luggage in, but there were none big enough, and I didn't have correct change. Therefore, I was unable to leave the station, and so I waited for about three hours for the others.

At last, I saw them. Mike was ill with some stomach bug. We waited on the station while Jill looked for a place for us to stay. Ultimately, we booked into the Flowers Hotel. Mike and Jill covered the bill, which they hoped to recover from Phillip.

For breakfast, I decided to challenge my stomach to a Burger King Whopper. I don't know why I did this, other than to boast that I had eaten at Burger King in Canada, the U.S., Britain, the Netherlands, Ireland, France and now Taiwan. I hadn't had a burger breakfast since I did an all night get-in for Theatre in the Park in Vancouver twenty years earlier. To my horror, the sales clerk cheerfully advised me that this was "two-for-one" day.

I told Jill "I'm going sight-seeing, and I'll see you back here later." "No," she said. "We're all going out to the airport as soon as possible." Why, for heavens sake? This is our last day! My last chance to see the National Palace Museum! "Because I don't want to worry about where everybody is."

Jill was doing her best Mother Hen impression, but I was not going to spend my last four hours in Taiwan waiting in an airport terminal. I stormed out of the hotel. For three months I had lived and worked under conditions that would have been illegal back home, because I wanted to travel and experience a different culture. But only Jill could change our tickets.

I never made it to the museum. Nor did I see a Chinese Opera. I walked across the street, taking the lift to the observation deck of Taipei's tallest building, the fifty-one story Shin Kong Life tower, for a view of the city and the surrounding mountains. When we caught the bus to the airport, I reminded Jill that we would probably be faced with an airport tax. "I know you're trying to be helpful", Jill blurted, "but you're really winding me up."

I stayed clear of her for the rest of the trip. Not only did we have to pay 300 NT in airport tax, but also a £35 administration charge for changing the booking on our ticket.

Vaughan nearly had to pay a further 3800 NT for overweight baggage, and he couldn't figure out why. Only after he opened his suitcase did he remember he had packed a telephone directory (!)

We met Chris at the airport. He had been hiding out at Camille's. I whispered in his ear that I had "arranged for a small piece of sh*t to hit the fan".

We were on our way home. We collectively clicked our heels together three times and said good-bye to cold rice dinners, long hours and crooked bosses, good-bye to smelly crowded Taipei and hello to smelly crowded London. A slight tinge of sadness came over me. We had left a job unfinished in a country that didn't realise how beautiful it could be.

Although I was paid for my last full week, New Aspect still owed me two days work plus about 2,000 NT[30] in cab fares, in addition to the transportation costs which they were bound by contract to pay. For that matter, they should have paid me my full wages through until 25 April. I accepted that I would never see that money. I got off lucky. Some others were still without their last week's wages.

---

[30] £40

As we came through Schiphol airport in Amsterdam, Kat's name was called over the public address system. It was Greg on the phone, asking her to marry him.

James Joyce once described "sentimentality" as "unearned emotion". When we arrived at Heathrow, I shrank into the background as everybody said their good-byes. I was not in a sentimental mood. Paul and I took the train in to Paddington Station. As soon as we found a shop, Paul, with the spirit of a man who had been deprived of the trappings of English civilisation for three months, announced, "I'm going to have a Mars bar." I elected for a Kitkat.

Encore:
The Cockroach Farm

Coming home was anti-climactic. I cushioned the adjustment by immediately booking myself on a cheap three-day mini-cruise to Spain. All the while, I felt like the Aussies in that Chinese shop. Everywhere I looked, nothing but white people. It must be a convention. But then again, I wondered if every Caucasian in Taiwan would now be asked, "Are you part of the circus?"

Then I had to face the task of finding a job. There were rumours that Phillip had more work for us, either in Egypt or Kuwait. In the meantime, as a temporary (with much emphasis) measure, I returned to my much-loathed security position. John, the Irishman, asked "Wot you dooin' wid da sor-cas? Wore you a sacyoraty gaard dere den?" "What happened?" said another, "Did the animals kick you out?" I answered, quite truthfully, "Something like that."

My friends back home had followed my dispatches with intrigue. Laurie from Ladner, who had just returned from her own adventure teaching art to children in India, wrote:

It was hard for me to read the parts about the animals. I hate seeing them being treated badly, especially when they are there to entertain us foolish humans.

Some other friends held a *"Mel Wrote" Place* party, sharing my dispatches.

The "small piece of sh*t" I told Chris about was the copy of my journal which I sent off to the *China News*, complete with photographs of the conditions the horses were being kept under.

The circus tried to struggle on, a pale reflection. They hoped to make up their losses over the Chinese New Year, but it was an uphill endeavour.

I soon settled into a new job backstage in a West End theatre. After a while, I received a message on my voice-mail to call a woman named Idelette from the *China News*. I thought, "Good, they've finally got around to me."

I called the first number she gave me, and a man answered "Wei" ("Hello")? I said I would like to speak to Idelette. "Okay!" he said. Then he put me on hold. For a long time. I checked my phone tariff book under Taiwan and it said £1.20 per minute off-peak. It was not off-peak. A shudder of déja vu came over me, and imagining that he was probably looking up "Idelette" in a dictionary, I hung up and tried the second number. I got an answerphone with an outgoing message in English. Getting warm, I thought.

A few hours later, she called me back and we talked for about twenty minutes. She told me that the show was still struggling on, albeit without Aladdin. They had played four more cities in the three months since we left them in Chia-yi, but as many more stops had been cancelled. They claimed to have played for over 300,000 people. The ticket prices ranged between 500 NT (£10) and 1800 NT (£36). Then, two weeks before the tour was intended to finish, the entire company greeted Hsu to a sit-in. At last they were united. Faced with living in tiny rooms with mouldy fridges and no closets, they refused to get off the bus. Gavin told the *China News* "We're not asking to live like Kings and Queens. We just expect to be treated like guest international artists... This guy treats me as if I'm twelve years old."

New Aspect was contractually obligated to pay for medical insurance. However, none of the workers who made claims for small injuries had been compensated. Although the company carried a policy worth 23 billion NT with Hsing Fu Insurance Company, Mr. Hsu refused to reimburse Tiger John for a leg injury because he had not submitted the paperwork, branding him a "trouble maker" and "unreasonable".

"I think the ball game is over", said one performer. Hsu was fined 300,000 NT by Taipei city council for not having proper sprinklers in the tent, and a further 50,000 NT for the inadequate cage the baby bear was kept in. The artists were sixty shows short of the two hundred they were guaranteed in their contracts, which also contained a clause which read "[In] case of closure of the establishment, the producer will have the right to annul this contract without further payments." When they saw the state of their hotel in Taipei, it was the last straw. They dubbed it the "cockroach farm".

One KMT legislator, representing the Jane Goodall Institute, campaigned for an amendment to the Wildlife Conservation Act to effectively ban animal circuses. "We think animals should be in nature, not in cages," he said.

The following day, Taipei's Bureau of Urban Development gave its approval for the show to go ahead.

Hsu announced extra dates to make up for the ones cancelled. Gavin remarked, "I'll only believe it when I do it".

Idelette van Papendorp's article appeared in the *China News* on 5 April 1998. She quoted my journals extensively, especially the accounts of the attack on Chris and of the condition of the horses. A picture of the makeshift stable was discreetly credited as "File Photo" (when I sent it to them, they "filed" it before they printed it.) Somehow, the story of the sea lion death was leaked.

Simon returned to Taiwan. Even Chris, with a threat of violence hanging over him, had gone back to be with Camille.   True love weighs.   The circus finished in Taipei's Neihu district on 19 April 1998.

Epilogue:

Dancing Hsu's

In May 1998 I received a call on my mobile phone. "It's Paul." Who? "Paul. From Taiwan." He was on London's South Bank with Greg, Tom and Gedda putting up a tent for the Royal National Theatre's touring production of *Oh! What A Lovely War*.

We met up the next morning. Greg and Kat were now living in South London, and had a baby girl named Mayan Olivia.

Paul was still owed money by Phillip, who had put Caseload Ltd., the company through which he'd recruited us, into voluntary liquidation. No doubt he took a bath on the whole adventure. Due to the rantings of Saddam Insane, the Kuwait tour never happened. I spoke briefly to Louise at Phillip's office. I asked her if everybody – human and animal – made it safely out of Taiwan. She blandly replied that they did, but was no more forthcoming than usual. Martin the Gnome was later spotted working on one of

Phillip's shows in London. It was rumoured that Sweetpea had contracted Hepatitis C from one of the *Lady Boys of Bangkok* (another Gandey production). Christina Campolongo realised her ambition of becoming an acrobat, doing an aerial ballet in silk for Cirque du Soleil's *La Nouba* at Walt Disney World.

Years later, I was talking to a very eminent West End producer about the experience. When I mentioned Hsu's name, her face took on a "Slowly-I-turn,-step-by-step" expression. "I know Hsu Po-yun very well!", she said. "He's totally mad." She had brought an English play to Taiwan with New Aspect in the late 1980s, and said that if she hadn't had the backing of a major institutional theatre, she would have been in real trouble. "Did you get your money?" she asked. Most of it, I replied. "That's more than I can say," she sighed. The kicker is, she also knew Phillip Gandey. If only they had talked...

Then in 2006, I received an email from an American drummer named David Cox who had been performing with the Great Moscow Circus in Taiwan under the auspices of New Aspect. "The show featured an extremely talented line-up from all over the world, and backed by a respected production company from Australia called Edgley Entertainment", he wrote. "Just as in your story, things unravelled right from the start. The animals were stuck in quarantine for a month. We averaged about 500 people in a 2000 seat tent for 6 weeks. Promotion of the show was minimal, and the promotion that we did was strange. For instance,

Hsu had another drummer and I play drum solos on top of scaffolding at a political rally, which I believe he organised. My group and all of the live musical entertainment from the circus was let go after the run in Taipei. The rest of the circus moved on to Tainan, and to cut costs the artists had to work in areas they were not contracted to work while staying in a brothel to save money for the company. And for the past three weeks, the ones who were sent home have been working on getting a significant amount of money owed to us. I'm not even sure the ones who are still there have been paid yet."[31] Then I received another email from Adriaan Gerber, a South African lighting technician with the same tour who told me, "I am trying to convince the rest of the crew that's left to stand together and force them into submission but they want consequent proof of the previous tours problems." He hoped that my story would provide that proof. "Our company manager, choreographer and tour manager [are] gone [as in fled out of the country] as well as the executive producer and producer... We are working on bare minimum at the moment with set-ups and running of our show. Myself and the electrician ... have to buy supplies to keep going with our own money – even essentials like diesel and lamps while the Taiwanese are still trying to rip us off by giving us low quality everything."[32] Talk about déjà vu.

I've suffered occasional abuse from people who are opposed to animal circuses. Somebody with

---

[31] Email dated 6 December 2006.
[32] Email dated 11 December 2006.

the handle "Little Miss Butterfly" sent me an unsolicited email saying, "You know what you really need to do? Go to the PETA[33] circus [web] page, and see what suffering those animals would have been going through in that supposedly wonderful circus you toured with." Where did I ever say it was "wonderful"?

Although I think Little Miss Butterfly probably subscribes to the Politically Correct Cause of the Month, I must concede that I saw a lot of things that disturbed me, and I've begun to wonder, is a bear in a tutu really that amusing? While I believe zoos serve a useful educational purpose, it is harder and harder for me to defend animal circuses. It was a relief to return to the more culturally nourishing world of the theatre.

In some ways the experience is richer in memory than it seemed to be at the time. For every Hsu Po-Yun, there was at least one Wu Huey-shin. As my friend James Sherman said, "Running away and joining the circus is just a metaphor for the adventurous child in all of us."

Many cliché stories have been told of some young man going out into the world on a wild adventure, "drinking in life", taking drugs unknown even to qualified chemists and receiving wisdom at the bosom of some superannuated courtesan, thus emerging as a "complete person". I would bear no such clichés. But still, I learned some basic lessons:

---

[33] People for the Ethical Treatment of Animals

that the one thing about me that God did not value was my opinion.

The whole Taiwan odyssey is now a distant dream, and I don't think about it very often. The economic crisis that had engulfed Asia had not yet hit Taiwan when we were there. In fact, the pundits were praising Taiwan's economic miracle. This seemed puzzling when we were struggling against politicians, Triads and miscommunication while vying to put up a tent in the mud. But as I explored the country, I noticed that there was a lot of money flying around. The place was celebrating its new democracy. Seventy years earlier, it had been a Japanese colony. Forty years ago, it was a third world country, exporting cheap textiles. Thirty years ago, it was still under martial law. Now, ten years into its democracy, it had re-invented itself as the fastest growing economy in Asia, and its standard of living was fast overtaking Britain's. Even in the small villages, there were internet cafes on every street corner. They were a force to be reckoned with.

Fast forward to three years later: I was standing in Times Square, New York, with my brother-in-law Bill. "This looks like a city on steroids!" he said looking up at the skyscrapers (all of which were still standing at the time). It was six o'clock in the evening, and my show was supposed to start in two hours' time. Looking for a place to eat, we decided to forego Sardi's and Joe Allen's, settling instead for a quick pizza at Sbarro. This was my New

York debut as a musical theatre writer, and Bill had extended his holidays so that he could be there.

As we finished our dinner, we headed off down Broadway toward the theatre. We passed the houses where *Cats* and *Les Misérables* were playing, then turned east down Forty-third Street, walking toward Ninth Avenue. Although the theatre was located near Times Square, I must tell you that my show, *Oh Pioneers!* was not actually playing on Broadway. In fact, it turned out to be a tiny room up above an Italian restaurant. But that didn't matter. Some time later, when another show of mine called *A Little Princess* opened in the same city, the *New York Times* would say, "Mel Atkey has written lovely music"[34]. At last, a job with real cachet. And it didn't involve standing in the mud. This was my moment in the sun. After two decades of struggling, I had finally made it – to the starting gate.

---

[34] New York Times, Friday 7 November 2003

Then I learned that Cynthia got married...

Bibliography:
Reminisces of Hsu Ping and Hsu Po-yen, Institute of Modern History, Academia Sinicia, Taipei, 1996. (In Japanese)
Ned Williams, *Fairs and Circuses in the Black County*

Mel Atkey

Author

Mel Atkey has written three other books, *When We Both Got to Heaven* and *Broadway North: The Dream of a Canadian Musical Theatre*, both published by Natural Heritage Books, and *A Million Miles from Broadway – Musical Theatre Beyond New York and London*, published by Friendlysong. He has contributed articles to various magazines, newspapers (and one academic journal) in his native Canada. He has worked in radio and television as a broadcaster, but his first love is musical theatre, a subject on which he has lectured internationally. He was a finalist in the International Musical of the Year Competition in Aarhus, Denmark, in 1996, and has been short-listed for the *Vivian Ellis* and *Ken Hill Prizes*, the *Quest for New Musicals* and *Musical Stairs*. His first recorded song, "Far Away" received airplay on radio across Canada and the United States, and he has written music on commission for CBC Radio and for the 1989 Canada Day Celebrations in Vancouver. He made his New York debut in 2001 with the Off-Broadway musical *O Pioneers!* with book by Robert Sickinger. He and Sickinger's second collaboration, *A Little Princess*, opened in 2003. Mel Atkey is a writer associate of Mercury Musical Developments, and a member of the Writers' Union of Canada. He is now based in London, England.